food lovers
europe

A Celebration of Local Specialties, Recipes & Traditions

Cara Frost-Sharratt

gpp

Contents

Map of featured food lovers' destinations

Numbers correspond to those listed in the Contents (*see pages 2–3*).

FINLAND

RUSSIA

49

38

31
ESTONIA

LITHUANIA

30

POLAND

29

H
LIC

SLOVAKIA

28

32

HUNGARY

ROMANIA

OATIA

34

BULGARIA

35

38

TURKEY

GREECE

37

36

INTRODUCTION

ABOVE Campo dei Fiori is the oldest market in Rome.

OPPOSITE A cheese farm in Provence. Many cheese farms in the area are open for tours and tastings.

WHERE TO EAT CATEGORIES

Restaurants have been allocated as ✪, ✪✪ or ✪✪✪ according to the average cost of a meal within the particular city or region. As prices vary enormously between countries, it would be impossible to provide a definitive price band for all restaurants in Europe. Instead, the guide is intended to reflect average prices for a restaurant meal in each particular country.

✪✪✪ A Michelin-star restaurant or a local hotspot where you should expect to blow the budget.

✪✪ A mid-range or slightly more expensive restaurant.

✪ A restaurant that offers particularly good value for money.

Europe has one of the largest population densities and is a great influence on world events and politics. However, while there's a huge variety of languages and cultures, there's a strong commonality between the different countries, not least due to a shared history, quirky cultural similarities and constant migration.

Although Europe's landmass is relatively small, the actual topography is surprisingly diverse. It includes peninsulas, islands, mountain ranges, deserts, lakes, lagoons and forests with an equally varied climate, ranging from alpine chills to the balmy heat of the Mediterranean, all of which has helped shape the many different cultures and lifestyles. However, trying to divide Europe into separate regions isn't easy, and while we all refer to Southern and Northern Europe etc., it's still not universally agreed exactly where one region ends and another begins. And to add to the confusion, some people also refer to Central Europe, arguing that it has its own distinct culture. But, no matter which way you look at it, the fact remains that Europe is ultimately a whole, made up of many fascinating and wonderful parts.

Food, Glorious Food

Food is the great unifier. It doesn't just transcend different nations but also the peoples within each country. In fact, so many early childhood memories are based around food that it is no great surprise that cooking and eating play such an important part in the many different cultures. All the senses are involved in the process of eating and any one of them can be awakened later in life in a split second, whether by a specific taste or aroma from a cooking pot, the sight of a long-forgotten ingredient in a market or the sound of banter around the dining table.

Such memories are often linked to the happiest, most meaningful or most poignant events or stages in a person's life. Births, deaths, marriages, family gatherings, celebrations, commiserations, farewells and returns are often marked by large meals or special recipes. In Eastern Europe *babka* cake is traditionally served at Easter, *gravad lax* is a popular Christmas food in Scandinavia and stollen is a festive cake in Germany. Hundreds of other dishes are lovingly prepared for memorable meals on special days and a great number have been passed down through the generations, acting as a unifying culinary heritage.

The Culture of Cuisine

International travel is now faster and more frequent than ever, with people introducing their favorite foods to different parts of the world. Consequently, national cuisines are constantly evolving, and rightly so. This has happened all over Europe, sometimes with incredible speed, as countries have become more accessible, joined the EU, welcomed new restaurants, catered to tourists from across the world and

delighted in new foods and flavors. Yet despite these gradual changes, ancient traditions and ingrained food memories will always prevail, and this important facet of social and cultural history helps define the unique identity of each country.

Food Lover's Paradise

The sheer diversity of the different foods found across Europe makes this continent an absolute delight for the gourmet traveler. Whether you are visiting a number of different countries, choosing one region to explore or simply taking a city break, there is a wealth of good food to discover. Farmers' markets are prominent across the continent, but their scope and personality change dramatically from country to country. The utilitarian markets of the squares in Central and Eastern Europe are in stark contrast to the bijou and gourmet markets of the burgeoning London outdoor shopping scene. And while the dazzling colors and precise displays of the Provence markets make them the most famous on the continent, Paris holds its own with its ability to provide fresh market produce on a scale that renders supermarkets superfluous.

Whichever country, city or region you visit, the local market can be a wonderful experience. It is no-holds-barred shopping with the niceties of the high-end food emporium stripped away. There is lively banter and the tactile experience of food, free from vacuum packaging and supermarket uniformity. Markets allow producers to meet their customers and customers to get one step closer to the source of their food. Such markets are where you'll discover local specialties, seasonal produce and artisan foods. A trip to the market is essential, whether to buy the ingredients for a quick sandwich or a seven-course gastronomic feast.

Off the Beaten Track

Away from the marketplace, canny food lovers will be in their element in Europe. The UK has taken the concept of the farmers' market directly to the farm and many have now opened up shops on site, selling produce and meat just yards from where it was grown and raised. Such shops range from small counters tucked away in farm buildings to state-of-the-art barn conversions, with other local producers being given a chance to sell their products, increasing the range on show. The Slow Food Movement also has a number of farm shops across the continent. The organization shuns the fast-food lifestyle and has been rapidly spreading across Europe, attracting like-minded producers. Since being founded in Bra, Italy, in 1986, it has found a captive audience among those looking for more sustainability and openness in food production.

In addition, in Central Europe artisan breweries are making a comeback, producing fine ales and beers in the traditional way. Beer halls, microbreweries and brewpubs enable customers to see how their drinks are made. Similarly, wineries around the continent are busy producing world-class wines on estates both large and small. Many vineyards offer tours and tastings, and the Loire Valley, Porto and Rhineland are just some of the destinations offering wine lovers the opportunity to taste some of the best varieties in Europe. And don't forget, festivals take place in most small villages in the wine-producing regions where you can sample the local produce. In fact, there are festivals in Europe for every

ABOVE *Cured hams hanging from ceilings are a common sight all over Spain.*

NOTES ON RECIPES

Both metric and US customary units are given for the recipes. Follow either set of measures, not a mixture of both, as they are not interchangeable.

Underneath the recipe title, the place of origin of the recipe is given. Where a dish is characteristic of the country rather than a specific region or city it is described as "classic."

food imaginable: truffles are celebrated in Alba, soup in Budapest and regional cheeses in Catalonia.

Destination Europe

There are so many exciting food destinations in Europe that selecting the best has been no easy task. And while a city or region might be famous for one aspect of its cuisine, a destination needs to offer the gourmet traveler the whole package. Regional specialties might mark out a place as being worthy of note but restaurant accolades demonstrate the staying power of a city or region as a hub of culinary creativity and greatness. Artisan producers, noteworthy delicatessens, butchers of distinction and locally renowned cafes and eateries that have remained under the tourist radar help transform a place of foodie interest into a fully fledged gourmet destination.

As we dine out more, take more foreign holidays and pay more attention to the quality of our food, our expectations of restaurants and shops has increased. We have become more blasé about

experiences that would have delighted and impressed those from just a generation or two back, and our standards concerning choice, presentation, flavor and service are now very high. This makes it even more difficult for a destination to stand out and impress serious food lovers. However, the following European cities and regions (some well known, others more surprising) clearly demonstrate the breadth and diversity of culinary excellence.

Author's Note

I have based the chosen destinations on a variety of criteria – subjective and objective – in an attempt to uncover the hidden gems of food lover's Europe. I have trawled my memory, photographs and numerous notebooks. I have pounded the streets, pestered friends, tried out recipes and revisited favorite shops, bars and cafes. I have combined my two passions of food and travel to write the sort of guidebook that I would like to read myself if I were embarking on a gourmet trip to the continent. But, if foreign travel is a pipe dream, I hope that the book can still provide inspiration, evoke fond memories or act as a wish list of places to go, restaurants to book and food to try on your next holiday.

The destinations have been divided up by country, with a brief introduction to the history, culture and food of the region, as well as some basic travel information for quick reference. The destinations themselves include descriptive text followed by personal recommendations for shops, food producers, restaurants and events that shouldn't be missed. There are also some recipes included. I hope you enjoy reading the book as much as I've enjoyed researching and writing it.

PORTUGAL

PORTUGAL IS A well-known holiday destination and sun worshipers flock to the resorts of the Algarve for their annual break. However, for the more intrepid traveler willing to scratch just below the surface of the sandy beaches and tourist menus, Portugal is a diverse and fascinating country with an illustrious history and a unique cuisine. You don't have to travel too far from the tourist trail of the Algarve to discover a country that is steeped in history, religion and tradition. Ancient farming methods are still employed in the Minho region, while the vast Alentejo is characterized by endless open space, dotted with reminders of the Moorish occupation of the area.

The food of Portugal is inextricably linked to its history, as well as the geography and diversity of the various regions. Yet, despite the many distinct flavors, recipes and ingredients that characterize the disparate geographical locations, there are certain keynotes in the Portuguese larder that truly reflect this distinctive and exciting cuisine. The lengthy Atlantic coastline means fresh fish and seafood are in abundance, salt cod is a national obsession, pastries are the sweet indulgence of choice and port is a national source of pride. Visitors are now beginning to fully appreciate the food and drink that the Portuguese have enjoyed for centuries.

travel essentials

TIME ZONE: GMT
TELEPHONE CODE: +351
CURRENCY: Euro
CAPITAL: Lisbon
LANGUAGE: Portuguese

GETTING THERE: Portugal has three main airports – Lisbon, Porto and Faro – all offering international services. A number of major seaports mean that it is possible to arrive by ferry or cruise ship, while the land border with Spain offers plenty of options for rail travel from other European destinations. Eurotunnel and various ferry services to France and Spain have made driving from other countries a viable option.

Douro

The mighty Douro River is at the heart of this northern region of Portugal, and it has accounted for the success of the area in terms of trade and wealth for hundreds of years.

ABOVE Taylor's port, one of the best-known producers in the region.

OPPOSITE Stock up on all your grocery provisions at the famous Mercado do Bolhão.

Douro is the home of port wine, and the fertile land of the lengthy river valley and adjacent hillsides are where the remarkable journey from grape to bottle begins. The landscape is an endless picture postcard of well-tended vineyards (*quintas*) where this ubiquitous Portuguese product is lovingly and passionately produced.

The city of Porto, the second-largest city in Portugal, remains intrinsically linked to making port and is a natural base for visitors. However, besides its tie to fortified wine, it is a cultural and gastronomic haven, offering a compact insight into the food and culture of the region. Towns such as Vila Nova de Gaia and Mesão Frio are more culinary gems.

Specialties and Local Producers

It's impossible to talk about Douro without mentioning some of the great port producers of the region. Vineyards abound but Taylor's is one of the most internationally recognized names, and the company has a number of wineries. Many *quintas* offer tours and tastings, and this is the best way to become better acquainted with the diversity and sheer scale of port production in the Douro valley. For greater immersion in this regional specialty, head to one of the historic vineyards, such as Quinta do Vale Meão or Offley.

Although port is the jewel in the crown of Douro, there are many other culinary highlights that are worthy of mention and sampling. The cities of Chaves and Lamego produce acclaimed smoked sausages and ham, including the dry-cured *presunto* ham, which is known throughout the country. The city of Mirandela is proud of its chicken sausages (*alheira*), while back in Porto the Portuguese staple ingredient of salt cod is used to make a dish that is a specialty of the city. The hearty casserole, known as *bacalhau à Gomes de Sà*, is now a firm favorite all over Portugal.

3 things you **must not** miss

◀ 1 Port Wine Tour
Head across the Douro River to Vila Nova de Gaia for a tour of the big names in port. Local tourist offices will help create your ideal route. www.cellartours.com

2 St. John's Festival
This midsummer celebration is a riot of noise, color and music and is the biggest festival of the year in Porto. Barbecue stands offer plenty of opportunities for eating on the go. www.gooporto.com

3 Quinta do Portal Winery
Get up close and personal at one of the best Douro wineries by taking a tour and then stay overnight in the stunning winery guest house. www.quintadoportal.com

WHERE TO EAT

D.O.C.
Estrada Nacional, 222
5110-204 Folgosa
Armamar
t +351 254 858 123
w www.restaurantedoc.
com/pt

*Celebrated chef Rui Paula is
at the helm of this trendy
restaurant in the heart of
port country. The views and
the food are to die for.*

D. TONHO
Cais da Ribeira, 13–15
4050-509 Porto
t +351 222 004 307
w www.dtonho.com

*This riverside eatery in the
center of Porto is a treat for
the eyes and the taste buds,
with great views over the
city and surrounding area.*

O RESTAURANTE
TRIPEIRO
Rua Passos Manuel, 195
4000-385 Porto
t +351 222 005 886

*As the name suggests, the
dish of the day is tripe. This
is the place to sample the
local specialty and they
serve it in a number of
different ways.*

Markets and Shops

As befits a region based on wine production, there is no shortage of places in which to sample and purchase the best that the Douro has to offer. In Porto, Vinoteca is the place to discover the best regional wines. Vinho e Coisas is located just outside Porto in Matosinhos and is stocked with an incredible variety of Portuguese wines.

With all this wine and port, it would be easy to overlook the food but luckily there are constant reminders of the gastronomic wonders of the Douro valley in the form of generously stocked markets and shop windows piled high with sweet treats. You can find all of the following in Porto. The Mercado do Bolhão is perhaps the best known of the Douro markets and is certainly the liveliest. It is a vast, covered market that is open daily and sells everything from fish to flowers. For a truly food-related shopping experience in the city, the Mercado de Porto Bolco is dedicated solely to goings on in the kitchen. For some sophisticated retail therapy, take a trip to MUUDA. This concept shop showcases Portuguese designers and features goods under the umbrella of "art, food and design." If you have time, you can stop for lunch or a sushi-making workshop.

Lisbon

Lisbon is both the largest city in Portugal and its capital. It is perched at the southern tip of the Estremadura region, where the Tagus River flows out to meet the Atlantic Ocean.

WHERE TO EAT

RESTAURANTE ELEVEN
Rua Marquês de Fronteira
Jardim Amália Rodrigues
1070 Lisbon
t +351 21 386 2211
w www.restaurant
   eleven.com

This minimalist eatery uses seasonal ingredients to produce some of the best dishes in town.

CLARA
Campo Mártires da Pátria,
   No 49
1150-225 Lisbon
t +351 21 885 3053
w www.lisboa-clara.pt

Escape to this quiet, decadent corner of Lisbon to indulge in some traditional dishes with a hint of international flavors.

CAFÉ A BRASILEIRA
Rua Garrett, 120, Chiado
1200 Lisbon
t +351 21 834 69541

This historic cafe is something of a Lisbon institution. Well worth a visit for its sumptuous decor and delicious custard tarts.

As the capital of Portugal, Lisbon enjoys the gastronomic bounty that the rest of the country has to offer because it acts as a natural confluence for the many regional specialties. However, it also remains staunchly dedicated to the preparation and enjoyment of its indigenous foodstuffs, and to the culinary highlights of the city and surrounding area.

Lisbon was one of the most important ports in the world during the 16th and 17th centuries. Food was inextricably linked to its success, with spices and other exotic ingredients being brought here from the New World. This legacy of travel and discovery, combined with the many cultures that have left an imprint on Lisbon, have resulted in a cuisine that acts as a historical and cultural timeline, which is both traditional and contemporary.

Specialties and Local Producers
While some regions indulge in their specialty dishes to the point of excluding neighboring fare, Lisbon has a history of embracing the diverse range of food and drink from all over the country, and indeed the world. However, the city is still proud of its local producers and the wide choice available to its inhabitants has by no means made them lackadaisical towards home-produced food.

Grilled sardines are one of the great specialties of Lisbon and they are hungrily

3 things you **must not** miss

1 Lisbon Festival
You can enjoy authentic grilled sardines and dance to traditional *fado* music at this massive street party held in June. *www.visitlisboa.com*

2 Solar do Vinho do Porto
The palatial setting of the Port Wine Institute is impressive enough, but it pales into insignificance when faced with the heady selection of over 300 ports. *www.ivp.pt*

▶ 3 Lisbon Fish and Flavors
This annual festival is a celebration of all things gourmet and it offers the chance to see the top chefs in the city demonstrate their culinary prowess. Cookery demonstrations, classes and wine tastings. *www.peixem lisboa.com*

devoured during the sardine season, from May until October. This simple delicacy is so prolific that it's difficult to avoid sampling it. Corner stalls, cafes and restaurants around the city release a mouth-watering aroma of the gorgeous grilled fish, which is impossible to ignore. Cake lovers are also seduced by another Lisbon recipe. The dangerously delicious little custard tarts, known as *pastéis de nata* (see page 16), originated in the Jerónimos Monastery in the city. The nuns cooked and sold them on the premises but they proved so popular that they soon appeared in every cafe in Lisbon. Today, it is widely agreed that Antiga Confeitaria de Belém is the place to get the best pastries.

Food is generally accompanied by drink and the tipple of choice in Lisbon is the locally produced *ginjinha* liqueur. Made by soaking sour cherries (*ginja*) in brandy, the monks of the São Domingos convent first produced the drink on a large scale.

Markets and Shops
Lisbon provides the ideal combination of ease and unexpected discovery when it comes to food shopping, and has some fantastic food markets. Mercado da Ribeira is a vast, covered market that is open daily, selling all manner of foodstuffs and other

items while Rua de São Pedro is the place to go for fish. Every morning, this narrow street turns into a fish market with stalls crammed along its length.

For gourmet treats, head to Mercearia da Atalaia in Bairro Alto, a grocery store with a delectable selection of some of the finest wine, cheese, pâté and chocolate. If sardines are the only items on your shopping list, take an empty bag to Conserveira de Lisboa and feast your eyes on floor-to-ceiling shelves piled high with canned fish.

OPPOSITE ABOVE Grilled sardines are a treat for all the senses.

OPPOSITE BELOW The Castelo de São Jorge dominates the skyline above the center of the city.

BELOW Salt cod croquettes are a popular snack in bars and cafes (see page 16).

Salt cod croquettes

Pastéis de bacalhau
SOUTHERN PORTUGAL

makes **12**

1 lb (450 g) salt cod
2 cups (600ml) milk
2 bay leaves
¾ lb (350 g) potatoes, peeled and chopped
2 oz (50 g) all-purpose flour, sieved
1 oz (25 g) ground almonds
Small handful of parsley, finely chopped
2 garlic cloves, grated
1 Tbsp capers, rinsed, dried and chopped
Freshly ground black pepper
4 Tbsp olive oil

Place the salt cod in a bowl, cover with water and leave to soak for 24 hours. The water will need to be changed three times during this period.

Drain the cod and place in a large saucepan. Pour in the milk, add the bay leaves and heat until just simmering. Poach for 15 minutes. Set aside to cool then drain the fish, reserving the poaching liquid. Remove the skin and bones and flake it into a bowl.

Bring the poaching liquid to the boil in a pan, add the potatoes and cook for 10 minutes, or until tender. Drain and mash. Add the cod to the potatoes and mix. Then add the flour, almonds, parsley, garlic and capers and combine. Season with pepper.

Form the mixture into 12 small sausage-shaped croquettes and set aside to chill in the fridge for 20 minutes. Heat the oil in a frying pan over a medium heat and fry the croquettes until cooked through and golden. Serve immediately.

Custard tarts

Pastéis de nata
LISBON

makes **12**

Butter, for greasing
3 egg yolks
4 oz (100 g) superfine sugar
1 oz (25 g) cornstarch
1 vanilla pod, split and seeds scraped out
¾ cup (225 ml) milk
1 cup (225 ml) heavy cream
10 oz (300 g) ready-rolled puff pastry
All-purpose flour, for dusting

Preheat the oven to 350°F/180°C/gas mark 4.

Grease a 12-hole tart tray with butter. Whisk the egg yolks, then add the sugar and cornstarch and mix together. Pour into a large saucepan and stir over a medium heat, until it has thickened.

Add the vanilla seeds to the pan, reduce the heat slightly then pour in the milk a little at a time, stirring constantly. Gradually pour in the cream and constantly stir the mixture over a low heat. When the mixture has thickened again, increase the heat so that it just comes to the boil. Remove the pan from the heat immediately, cover and set aside.

Roll the pastry thinly on a floured work surface. Fold it in half and roll again. Roll it into a sausage shape then cut into 12 equal slices. Roll each slice into a thin circle and lightly press each one into the tin.

Stir the custard gently and divide the mixture between the pastry cases. Bake for 25–30 minutes. When ready, the pastry will be golden and the custard set.

SPAIN

THE CUISINE OF Spain is as surprising and varied as the landscape. With centuries of history involving transient cultures and peoples, Spain has developed a unique culinary identity that tells the story of its past while pushing the boundaries into the future.

Spanish food is characterized by hearty pans of paella and bean stew, bite-sized tapas, salads and vegetables liberally doused with olive oil, seafood fresh from the fisherman's net and the mighty Iberian hams from which delicate slivers of meat are cut. Everything is washed down with a selection of wine and cava, while sumptuous tarts and pastries round off the meal. Although modern Spain has carved an eclectic niche for itself in the culinary world, traditional, regional fare still holds its own, and the quality of the ingredients will undoubtedly ensure that these outstanding dishes stand the test of time.

travel essentials

TIME ZONE: **GMT +1**

TELEPHONE CODE: **+34**

CURRENCY: **Euro**

CAPITAL: **Madrid**

LANGUAGE: **Spanish**

GETTING THERE: Spain is easily accessible, with several international airports, and by train, boat or car. You can arrive overland through France or Portugal, and from the UK via Eurotunnel.

San Sebastián

While the rest of Spain has been quietly going about its business, San Sebastián has been earnestly building up its reputation as one of the most important food destinations in the world.

ABOVE San Sebastián is renowned all over Spain for its tapas.

RIGHT The streets of the city are packed with quality eateries serving traditional food.

OPPOSITE La Bretxa market is the hub of the San Sebastián shopping scene.

This beautiful city on the northeast coast of the Basque Country has Michelin stars sprinkled like confetti on its restaurants. The Basque pride in its culinary prowess is more than justified with the vast array of top-quality restaurants that line the streets. In fact, from snack bars to fine dining, everything is excellent. Throw in the beach, architecture, festivals and the stunning location and this is an idyll for anyone with a discerning palate and an eye for beauty.

Specialties and Local Producers

The Basque identity has had a huge influence on the style of cooking and the type of ingredients used in the kitchens of San Sebastián. The culture is firmly entrenched in food, and this has played a big role in the elevation of the city to gourmet superstardom. The disparate nature of the terrain, slowly evolving from sea to mountain, means that a vast range of ingredients and products can be produced in the region. Seafood is a specialty in San Sebastián, where the restaurants serve the fresh catch with the lightest of additions to bring out the natural flavors.

Typical Basque tapas (*pintxos*) are another speciality and San Sebastián is reputed to serve the best in the country. The etiquette in different bars varies and

3 things you **must not** miss

◀ **1 Wine Region Tour**
Tear yourself away from the gastronomic pleasures of the city center and explore the nearby vineyards of Txakoli. *www.cellartours.com*

2 Gastronomy Congress
A chance to invade the personal space of the biggest names in the San Sebastián culinary scene as top chefs gather to prove their worth. *www.sansebastiangastro nomika.com*

3 La Tamborrada Festival
The January drum festival offers the ideal opportunity to mix music with food. Let your ears take the strain when you're not ducking into tapas bars for a little light refreshment. *www.san sebastianturismo.com*

these tiny morsels of finger food are either available for you to help yourself or are made to order. The miniature food plates are usually matched with equally diminutive drinks in the form of tiny glasses of wine (*txikitos*). The aim is to sample a glass of wine and a couple of tapas from a number of different bars on an evening out. Wine isn't always on the menu, however, because the Basque Country is a famous cider-producing area.

Markets and Shops

It could almost be a culinary contradiction to travel to San Sebastián and then cook for yourself. With such a wide choice of high-quality eateries there seems little incentive to stay in and rattle pans. However, it would be even odder to bypass the wonderful markets, stalls and shops that help make the city a food lover's paradise. La Bretxa is the main market and is actually two buildings: one houses fresh produce while the other – La Pescadería – is the fish market. Both are well worth a visit and it is possible to buy virtually everything you need for classic Basque cuisine.

For dedicated carnivores, Zapore Jai is a well-known delicatessen stocking a mouthwatering selection of Iberian hams, as well as other choice products and ingredients. Vinataría Manu Méndez, in the Gros district, is a specialty wine shop with a choice of over 500 varieties.

WHERE TO EAT

• • • • • • • • • • • • • •

✕✕✕
ARZAK
Avenida Alcalde
   Elosegui, 273
20015 Donostia-
San Sebastián
t +34 943 278 465
w www.arzak.info

San Sebastián is the perfect place to sample Michelin-star meals and Arzak has it all – classy atmosphere, boundary-pushing food and faultless service.

✕✕
CASA VALLÉS
Reyes Católicos, 10
20006 San Sebastián
t +34 943 452 210
w www.barvalles.com

Relaxed yet intimate, Casa Vallés offers traditional Basque fare and seasonal specialties. You can nibble tapas in the bar or have a more leisurely meal in the restaurant downstairs.

✕
LA CEPA
Calle del Treinta y Uno
   de Agosto, 7
20003 Donostia-San
   Sebastián
t +34 943 426 394
w www.barlacepa.com

Enjoy the best Jabugo ham at this no-nonsense bar, which hails the mighty pig.

Galicia

Galicia juts out from the northwestern tip of Spain and its borders fringe land and sea. Vigo is the largest city in Galicia and has the largest fishing port in Europe.

ABOVE The tarta de Santiago is typically decorated with a Cross of the Order of Saint James.

OPPOSITE Mussel farms are a common sight along the coastline of Galicia.

Although this corner of the region is highly industrialized, much of Galicia is devoted to agriculture and farming and the food larders in this part of Spain are packed with great things. Tapas are very much in evidence here, and while rice and pasta are noticeable by their absence from many menus, the potato is the carbohydrate of choice, influencing many recipes.

Specialties and Local Producers

When travelling through Galicia it soon becomes apparent that seafood is the specialty. You will find mollusks, crustacea and shellfish of every conceivable variety, size and shape tossed in the cooking pot and miraculously transformed into delectable dishes, with octopus being the most highly respected dish. This is *the* regional meal, particularly when cooked with paprika (*pulpo a la gallega*).

With a large dairy industry, beef and cheese also feature heavily on the menu, particularly inland. A number of Galician products have achieved international acclaim and have Protected Designation of Origin status. Such products include the wonderful Cebreiro cow's-milk cheese, which is produced in Lugo and has a distinctive mushroom shape, and *queso Arzúa-Ulloa*, a handmade cheese with a creamy flavor. Another regional specialty is Saint James cake (*tarta de Santiago*). This rich almond tart is traditionally sold with a distinctive Cross of the Order of Santiago. Galicia is also a fairly prolific wine-producing region, with an impressive five demarcations to its name. These wines are increasingly making an impact on the international stage, including the highly acclaimed Albariño wines.

Markets and Shops

The medieval city of Santiago de Compostela sits inside Roman walls and is the perfect place to combine history and gastronomy,

3 things you **must not** miss

◄ 1 Cellar Tours
A chance to tour some of the fabulous vineyards in Galicia and enjoy the best wines of the region. *www.spainfood andwinetourism.com*

2 Galicia Seafood Festival
Take the opportunity to sample every possible variety of seafood during this popular October festival. *www.galinor. es/ogrove/index.html*

3 Arzúa Cheese Festival
Travel to Arzúa on the first Sunday in March and you'll discover thousands of varieties of cheese, including the town's own cheese, of which it is rightly proud. *www.concellodearzua.org*

⊗⊗⊗

CASA MARCELO

Rúa Hortas 1
15705 Santiago de
   Compostela
t +34 981 558 580
w www.nove.biz/ga/
   casa-marcelo

*Don't miss the innocuous
entrance. Step inside and
you'll find exquisite food and
smart service.*

⊗⊗

MESÓN DE ALBERTO

Calle Cruz 4
27002 Lugo
t +34 982 228 310
w www.mesonde
   alberto.com

*This legendary Lugo
establishment offers the
chance to enjoy tapas
downstairs, or treat yourself
to a gourmet dinner in one
of the upstairs dining rooms.*

⊗

ADEGA O BEBEDEIRO

Rúa Ángel Rebollo 34
15002 A Coruña
t +34 981 210 609
w www.adegao
   bebedeiro.com

*Sample some of the classic
dishes of the region in this
rustic restaurant that delivers
both quality and flavor.*

with its pavement cafes, miniature gardens and grand squares. The city is also the final destination of the epic pilgrimage, the Way of Saint James (Camino de Santiago). Many arrive at the cathedral weary but elated after walking for hundreds of miles.

The food market in the city is one of the best in the region. Situated in the old town, business is done as it has been for generations, with farmers and producers selling their wares directly to the public. Wine is to be found everywhere in the city and establishments such as Vinoteca O'beiro provide the opportunity to either sip on site or purchase bottles to take away. For an alcohol-free beverage stop, the Tea Shop offers a fine selection of all things tea and coffee related.

Travel a short distance to Lugo and your first stop should be Jamones Salvador, an opulent, upmarket delicatessen that, as its names suggests, specializes in ham.

Barcelona

With its iconic architecture, world-class restaurants and enviable beaches, Barcelona is one of the great cities of the world.

WHERE TO EAT

✪✪✪
MOO
Hotel Omm
Rosselló 265
08008 Barcelona
t +34 93 445 40 00
w www.hotelomm.es

With its modern twist on Catalan cuisine, this restaurant is stacking up well-deserved accolades for its wine and food, including a Michelin star.

✪✪
CERVECERÍA CATALANA
Carrer de Mallorca, 236
08008 Barcelona
t +34 93 216 03 68

This lively tapas restaurant is one of the best places to sample these little plates of flavor-packed food.

✪
QUIMET & QUIMET
Carrer del Poeta Cabanyes, 25
Barcelona
t +34 93 442 31 42

If you can squeeze into this tiny tapas bar you will be rewarded with tasty food and an incredibly impressive wine list.

It is certainly one of the most exciting for food, and it has recently been enjoying a great deal of attention because the combined creative genius of its top chefs has catapulted the city onto the culinary hot list.

Geographically, Barcelona is located in the northeast corner of the country. It is the capital city of Catalonia and the cultural heartland of Spain. It offers a frenzied assault on the senses with its fast-paced, 24-hour lifestyle, which seems to coexist with the more traditional elements of Spanish life. Nowhere is the juxtaposition between tradition and modernity more apparent than in the food. Tiny tapas bars rub shoulders with über-cool, cutting-edge restaurants while other venues slot happily in between.

Specialties and Local Producers

In Barcelona – like the rest of Spain – food is so much more than simply fuel, and the sights and smells of the markets demand the constant attention of the visitor. Two stalwarts of the Barcelona diet are cured meat and fresh seafood. Hams are treated with the same reverence as aged wines, with an almost ritualistic approach to carving and tasting. The ubiquitous sight of cured hams dangling from ceilings is common across the city, making Barcelona a carnivore's delight. The coastal location also ensures an abundant supply of seafood. Although not strictly a traditional

Barcelona dish, seafood paella does epitomize the abundance of seafood and the regard for authentic, traditional recipes and cooking techniques that have helped shape the city's cultural heritage.

Wine accompanies most meals in Spain and since Barcelona sits just to the north of Penedès, one of the major wine-producing regions in the country, a meal out provides the perfect opportunity to sample some local wines, such as Miguel Torres and Gramona.

Markets and Shops

You simply can't miss Barcelona's markets. Shopping in the city is as far removed from the anodyne supermarket experience as it's possible to get. The obvious starting point is La Boqueria market. Located in the heart of Barcelona, this immense covered collection of stalls satiates every possible food craving, while a number of innocuous-looking counters, such as El Quim de la Boqueria, serve fantastic fresh food. The recently refurbished Santa Catarina market offers an alternative and equally impressive choice of food. In fact, every neighborhood in the city has its own food market, and visitors are never far from stunning fresh produce.

On a smaller scale, a number of specialist food shops offer a vast range of Spanish specialties, displayed in carefully planned windows. Spanish nuns and monks are renowned for their quality foods and Caelum provides the opportunity to taste and purchase some of the best cakes, liqueurs and chutneys from around the country. Gourmet food shoppers must visit the superb delicatessen Colmado Quilez, while the best ham in town can be found at Jamonísimo and Can Ravell. The Formatgeria La Seu stocks a wide selection of Spanish farm cheeses, while sugar cravings can be indulged at the tempting Cacao Sampaka.

ABOVE La Boqueria market is a food lover's haven for both locals and tourists.

OPPOSITE LEFT Quality hams are the pride of Barcelona's cuisine.

OPPOSITE RIGHT La Seu Cathedral is just one of the many architectural highlights of the city.

3 things you **must not** miss

1 Escorted Market Tour

If your Spanish and Catalan language skills are limited, try joining an organized tour of La Boqueria. Expert guides help with transactions and information. *www.catalonia tours.com*

2 La Mercè

This September festival is the biggest in the Barcelona calendar. Prepare to immerse yourself in a weeklong celebration of music, culture and, of course, food. *www.bcn.cat/merce*

▶ 3 Chocolate Museum Tour

A must-see for anyone with a passion for chocolate. This large, contemporary space explores every aspect of chocolate production and history. *www.pastisseria.com/ en/portadamuseu*

Catalonia

Catalonia is one of the great food regions of Spain. As a close neighbor of south-east France, there is some overlap between the cooking traditions of the two areas.

ABOVE Olive groves dot the landscape of Catalonia.

RIGHT Palafrugell market is one of the best in the area with its vast array of fresh produce.

OPPOSITE In the evening Palafrugell's market stalls make way for restaurant tables and diners.

There is a huge sense of pride in Catalan food and cooking, and the distinctions between food here and in the rest of the country are marked, although there is also a great deal of cohesion. Due to its geographical location and its historical seafaring trade routes with North Africa and Italy, Catalonia was influenced long ago by foreign ingredients. Many have been subtly incorporated into dishes without detracting from the indigenous quality.

Today, Catalonia is at the heart of the modern Spanish food revival with chefs, such as Ferran Adrià, breaking the mold. This new breed of cooks is pushing the boundaries of Spanish cuisine, delivering familiar ingredients and flavors in a highly innovative way.

Specialties and Local Producers

Cava is a great source of pride in Catalonia. The sparkling wine was first produced in the

3 things you **must not** miss

◀ 1 Anis del Mono Distillery Tour
Discover the history of this famous Spanish liqueur with a tour of the distillery and a sample of this distinctive licorice-flavored drink.
www.badalona.cat/aj-badalona/turisme/es/itineraris/anismono.html

2 Sant Ermengol Fair
This celebration of regional cheeses in La Seu d'Urgell includes varieties from Catalonia as well as the Basque Country and France.
www.laseu.cat

3 Olive Oil Mill Tour and Tasting
Sample some of the finest extra-virgin oils in the country and learn how the precious liquid is extracted from the fruit.
www.epicureanways.com/trips/gourmetemporda/catalonia

region in the late 19th century and the industry is still flourishing with most of the wine coming from the Penedès area. A number of other wines are also produced here, many of which are exported and have helped to establish the reputation of Spain as a serious wine-producing nation.

The landscape of Catalonia is so diverse that animal rearing is as prolific as vine production. Olives also grow in abundance and some of the olive oils of Catalonia are highly regarded: Oli de l'Empordà is unfiltered extra-virgin oil that has been given Protected Designation of Origin status. It comes as no surprise that olive oil is so highly prized that the simple dish of bread and oil is a staple snack in Catalonia. *Pa amb tomàquet* is literally a few slices of bread rubbed with garlic and tomato, then drizzled with olive oil. Other fruit trees dot the landscape and Girona apples, in particular, are renowned for their flavor.

Markets and Shops

Catalonia is a large and diverse region with many culinary highlights and plenty of opportunities to buy local products. Food markets are held on a daily or weekly basis in towns and cities across the region. The daily indoor food market in Girona offers fresh meat, fish and other produce while other smaller markets and stalls are dotted around the city. For a glorious backdrop to the weekly shop, the medieval town of Pals has a weekly market, while the market in Palafrugell is one of the best in the area and includes fresh produce and fish. Back in Girona, the Chocolate Factory offers a range of sweet treats, while in the town of La Seu d'Urgell the well-known Formatgeria Casa Eugene is the place to indulge a passion for cheese. You can taste some of the exciting new cheeses that are emerging from the Catalan region.

WHERE TO EAT

EL CELLER DE CAN ROCA
Can Sunyer, 48
17007 Girona
t +34 972 222 157
w www.cellercanroca.com

This stylish restaurant demonstrates the evolution of Spanish cuisine with its varied menus and two Michelin stars.

JOAN GATELL
Passeig Miramar, 26
43850 Cambrils Port
E-tarragona
t +34 977 366 782
w www.joangatell.com

This is consistently lauded as the best restaurant experience in Catalonia. Great quality at justifiable prices.

CASA MARIETA
Plaça Independència, 5–6
17001 Girona
t +34 972 201 016
w www.casamarieta.com

The oldest restaurant in Girona offers simple, home-cooked fare prepared in the Catalan way.

Andalucía

The second-largest region in Spain has the largest population. It lies across the south of the country, the region's southernmost tip practically touching North Africa.

ABOVE The orange groves of Seville are famous the world over.

OPPOSITE The Alhambra Palace offers a fascinating insight into the history of Andalucía.

The food of the region constitutes some of the most diverse and exciting in the country, with the sheer size of the area and the different types of terrain and geographical features resulting in a cross-section of ingredients and specialties.

In the south, the lasting influence of the Moors is still obvious in the towns and cities. The Alhambra Palace in Granada is perhaps the best introduction to this extensive period of occupation that left a legacy of astonishing architecture, and more than a nod to the food and culture of North Africa. The regional capital of Seville is famous for its oranges but is more astonishing as a vibrant cultural hub whose buildings amaze and whose food surpasses expectations. Down on the coast, Málaga is a sprawling tourist magnet, dishing out a miniature version of Spain in varying degrees of authenticity. Travel to the eastern coast to the province of Almería and the coastal tourist towns give way to the ethereal, rocky inland landscapes; a far cry from sea and sangria but no less typical of this fascinating and exciting region.

Specialties and Local Producers

Andalucía is the proud home of the famous Spanish tapas. Although choices vary widely between the regions, this is definitely the place to sample some of the best and most authentic beer snacks in the country. When it comes to main courses, both meat and seafood vie for center stage. The lamb of Córdoba is renowned throughout Spain, and the endless coastlines supply restaurants and markets all over the region with a dizzying variety of wonderfully fresh fish and seafood. However, Jabugo ham is the prize draw for carnivores. This air-dried mountain ham is considered by many to be

3 things you **must not** miss

◄ 1 Seville Tapas Walking Tour
Tapas is an essential part of the Andalucía experience, and the best way to make the most of these delectable little bites is to visit a number of bars, taking in the ambience of each with a plate of tapas and a glass of beer or sherry. *www.andalucia.com/ gastronomy/tapas.htm*

2 Jerez Sherry Tour
Take a day out to visit a typical sherry bodega, including the vineyard and cellars and, of course, tasting the finished product. *www.cadizandbeyond.com/ jereztours/sherrytourtasting/ tabid/134/default.aspx*

3 Seville Fair
This two-week celebration in April is a chance to experience the best of Andalucían hospitality and culture through music, dancing, eating and drinking. *www.andalucia.com/festival/ seville-feria.htm*

WHERE TO EAT

✖✖✖
LA ALQUERÍA
El Bulli Hotel
41800 Sanlúcar la Mayor
Seville
t +34 955 703 344
w www.elbullihotel.com

This stunning hotel and restaurant in a converted Moorish farmhouse could come straight out of a fairy tale. La Alquería dutifully recreates the dishes for which Ferran Adrià gained fame in El Bulli, and has gained two Michelin stars.

✖✖
PARADOR DE GRANADA
Calle Real de la Alhambra s/n
18009 Granada
t +34 958 221 440
w www.paradores-spain.
    com/spain/pgranada.html

This restaurant in a luxury hotel is in the Alhambra itself. The food is a mix of Andalucían and Spanish classics, while the terrace offers tranquility and spectacular views.

✖
BAR JUANITO
Plaza de Vargas, 6
11403 Jerez de la Frontera
t +34 956 334 838
w www.bar-juanito.com

The town might be most famous for its sherry but the food is very good, too. This famous tapas bar attracts the crowds but that's no reason to avoid the authentic dishes that sum up the region in spades.

the best of its kind in the world. The ham is produced from Black Iberian pigs in a relatively small area fairly close to Seville, with the natural mountain air apparently giving it a finer flavor than other cured ham varieties.

If you're going to eat tapas and ham, you need an outstanding olive oil as an accompaniment, and Córdoba produces just that – a large amount of the country's oil made to exceptionally high standards. Sherry is another gemstone in Andalucía's culinary crown and there are many top-quality producers in the Cádiz region, where the production of this exclusively Andalucían fortified wine takes place. Like champagne, sherry has Protected Designation of Origin status and its production is tightly controlled.

Markets and Shops
Shopping is a delight throughout Andalucía, with huge food markets, smaller local organic markets, specialized shops and impromptu stalls by roadsides. In Seville there are a number of glorious food markets, their stalls groaning under the weight of local produce and delicacies. The market on Calle Feria is popular with local shoppers and Triana is about as typical a Spanish food market as you are likely to find. In Huelva the fish market is said to be one of the best in the region, and its location in this important port city ensures that the catch of the day arrives fresh. The stallholders in Ayamonte set up shop every day, while up in the beautiful mountain town of Órgiva, a thriving organic farmers' market reflects the burgeoning interest in organic food.

Cold vegetable soup

Gazpacho
ANDALUCÍA

serves **4**

2 slices of day-old bread, crusts removed
and cut into cubes
2 garlic cloves
2 lb (900 g) tomatoes, peeled, seeded
and chopped
2 onions, chopped
1 red pepper, seeded and chopped
1 green pepper, seeded and chopped
1 cucumber, peeled, seeded and chopped
½ cup (100 ml) extra-virgin olive oil
2 Tbsp (25 ml) white wine vinegar
¼ cup (50 ml) water
Salt and freshly ground black pepper

FOR THE GARNISH:
1 large tomato, peeled, seeded and diced
1 red or green pepper, seeded and diced
½ red onion, cut into small dice
½ cucumber, cut into small dice

Place all the soup ingredients into a food processor and purée until the mixture is thick and smooth.

Place a sieve over a large bowl and pour the soup through it. Place the soup in the fridge to chill, until ready to serve.

Prepare the garnish when ready to serve. Ladle the soup into serving bowls and place a little mound of the garnish on top of each one.

Shrimp in garlic

Gambas al ajillo
CENTRAL/SOUTHERN SPAIN

serves **4 as a tapas dish**

3 Tbsp olive oil
2 garlic cloves, finely chopped
9 oz (250 g) fresh raw shrimp, peeled
Pinch of dried chili flakes
Salt and freshly ground black pepper

Heat the oil in a large saucepan and add the garlic, quickly followed by the shrimp and chili flakes. Cook for about 4–5 minutes (depending on the size of the shrimp), until the prawns change color and are cooked through. Season with salt and pepper and serve immediately.

FRANCE

FRANCE IS ONE huge food destination and it is supremely difficult to identify and isolate specific regions or cities for their culinary prowess. The country has a worldwide reputation for its fine food, with regional produce and specialties being guarded with a sense of fierce pride. The real beauty of French cuisine lies in its diversity: it runs the entire gamut of styles. There are the rustic stews and cassoulets of Limousin and the Basque Country, the Mediterranean-inspired food of Provence, the foie gras- and truffle-dominated menus of Périgord and ultimate fine dining in Paris, Lyon and other cities.

France takes an inordinate amount of pride in its food. From a simple omelette (see page 40) to a multicourse tasting menu at one of the many three-Michelin-star restaurants, the quality of the ingredients, the skill of the chefs and the execution of the dishes combine to produce food that is consistently outstanding.

travel essentials

TIME ZONE: **GMT +1**

TELEPHONE CODE: **+33**

CURRENCY: **Euro**

CAPITAL: **Paris**

LANGUAGE: **French**

GETTING THERE: France is easily accessible from all over the world. Many of its regional airports offer international flights, or easy transfers from larger cities around the country. The SNCF train network includes high-speed rail links between major destinations and also to other European countries, while Eurostar provides direct access from the UK.

Champagne-Ardenne

Although most noted for its exclusive and much-protected sparkling white wine, there is so much more to discover in this delightful part of the country.

ABOVE For the locals, Ardennes pâté and other regional specialties are as important as champagne.

OPPOSITE The lighthouse in the village of Verzenay is a well-known landmark on the Champagne Trail. It houses the Musée de la Vigne.

Champagne is an ancient region with a rich agricultural inheritance still intact. The land is lush and fertile and the food hearty and rustic. Despite the glamorous tags attached to the region's most famous export, the area is refreshingly down-to-earth and workaday. People go about their business in the many bustling market towns and the glitz of the sparkling aperitif lifestyle is at best understated across most of the area. In fact the region is most noted in France for its barley, wheat and onions.

Specialties and Local Producers

The Ardennes *département* is famous for its pâté, which is made from wild boar, indicative of the wild terrain and dense forests of the locale and its hunting culture. The white sausage, *boudin blanc*, is another local specialty and is made from pork, egg and milk. In the south of the region, the mild and creamy Langres cheese has received worldwide acclaim. Other cheeses, including

Chaource and Brie de Meaux, are also known outside France with Brie being one of the specialties of the Champagne region.

As for the famous drink, only sparkling wine produced in this region of France has the legal right to be called champagne. There are over 100 producers and many are household names, including Moët & Chandon, which only produces vintage champagne in especially good years, and Dom Pérignon (one of the most famous brands). It takes its name from the Benedictine monk who was influential in the production of sparkling wine in the region and introduced a number of processes that helped to preserve wine. A lot of champagne production is based close to the cathedral city of Reims and it seems fitting that another regional speciality, *biscuits de Reims*, should be so closely associated with the sparkling wine. These delicate pink biscuits are dipped in champagne before being eaten.

3 things you **must not** miss

◀ 1 Chaource Cheese Museum

Visit the town with the same name as the great cheese it produces and take a trip to the museum to find out more. *www.chaource.fr*

2 Champagne Fair

This annual week-long event is held in Troyes in June. Champagne and local food attract thousands of visitors. *www.tourism-troyes.com*

3 Champagne Trail

Take a leisurely drive along the well-signed champagne route, stopping for tastings and cellar tours at prestigious producers. *www.tourisme-champagne-ardenne.com*

Markets and Shops

Wherever you happen to be in the Champagne-Ardenne region, you can assume that there will be a farmers' market somewhere close by every day of the week. The covered market in Reims has been plying its produce to customers for hundreds of years. Épernay is in the heart of champagne country and the four market places provide plenty of opportunity to stock up on food, drink and crafts. The beautiful walled city of Langres is a delightful spot to stock up on fresh fruit and vegetables.

Heading back to Reims, there is every opportunity to purchase the accompaniments to a vintage bottle of champagne and, naturally, a good deal of choice. The city has a number of quality delicatessens, including the 100-year-old Comtesse de Barry, which stocks everything from foie gras to cakes and a good selection of bubbly. The artisan La Chocolaterie Thibaut in Pierry allows visitors to combine some of the best chocolate and champagne that the region has to offer because this town is also home to great champagne producers, such as Vollereaux.

WHERE TO EAT

LE PARC, CHÂTEAU LES CRAYÈRES
64, bd Henry Vasnier
51100 Reims
t +33 3 26 24 90 00
w www.lescrayeres.com

Treat yourself to a meal at this stunning spot in Reims where the best in French cuisine is presented with panache.

LA BRASSERIE DU BOULINGRIN
48, rue de Mars
51100 Reims
t +33 3 26 40 96 22
w www.boulingrin.fr

Enjoy classic bistro dining in this historic art deco building. The food is exactly what you'd expect from a quality brasserie.

RESTAURANT BISTROQUET
Place Langevin
Troyes
t +33 3 25 73 65 65
w www.bistroquet-troyes.fr

The food is traditional Champagne-Ardenne fare in this little restaurant with plenty of ambience in the center of Troyes.

Paris

The capital of France is considered the food capital of the world. With its unrivaled access to the best produce, the city distributes, sells and cooks these ingredients around the clock in high style.

ABOVE Marché Raspail is the market of choice for Parisian celebrities.

RIGHT Poilâne bakery is famous for its ornately decorated loaves of bread.

OPPOSITE The relaxed cafe culture of Paris is apparent on every street corner.

In fact Paris collates much-beloved regional specialties from the far corners of the country and replicates them in the plethora of restaurants in its 20 *arrondissements*, or districts. These ingredients and dishes have been joined by many more from around the world as the cosmopolitan nature of the city has spread to the dining table, creating an exciting explosion of international flavors. Parisians are well aware of their enviable gastronomic inheritance and food is treated with the utmost respect whether they're shopping for groceries, enjoying a *menu du jour* at a local bistro or indulging in Michelin greatness.

Specialties and Local Producers

The old saying "don't keep a dog and bark yourself" could be applied to Parisian food. With the freshest and best-quality ingredients from around the country available all over the

3 things you **must not** miss

◀ 1 Grape Harvest Festival
Only the Parisians could manage to keep a successful vineyard running in the center of a city. This annual October festival celebrates the harvest from Montmartre and other local areas. *www.montmartre-paris-france.com*

2 Paris Food Walking Tour
Get to know the city and its food in intimate detail as you check out markets and sample some of the best wine and cheese in specialty shops. Various companies operate tours. *www.viator.com*

3 Dine at a Supper Club
The perfect opportunity to meet people and enjoy real home cooking at one of these impromptu "restaurants at home," which are springing up all over the city. *www.hkmenus.com*

city, there is little need to produce them here. However, despite the close proximity to the origin of much of their food, Parisians are insistent that certain products must be made in situ. Bread is baked in batches throughout the day by bakeries around Paris and is bought fresh every morning, if not for each meal. Jet-lagged baguettes are simply not an option and the city is teeming with artisan bakers dedicated to producing the best loaf in the locale. Among these is the award-winning Grenier à Pain in the Montmartre district, and Poilâne, which has two shops in the city and sells distinctive loaves decorated with flower motifs.

Parisians are also passionate about chocolate but, as with all the food they consume, only the best will do. This discerning sweet tooth has resulted in a disproportionate number of world-class chocolatiers working magic with cocoa and displaying their produce in gorgeously appointed shops. Michel Chaudun is one of the best-known names among chocoholics. As well as superb artisan confectionery, he is also famous for creating incredible chocolate sculptures. Other chocolatiers honing their craft in Paris include Jean-Paul Hévin and Christian Constant.

Markets and Shops

Daily shopping for fresh produce is such an intrinsic part of French life that markets are squeezed into pockets of every district of the city, and the only distinction between markets here and in the rest of the country is that some are doused in a generous helping of Parisian chic. Marché Raspail, on the Left Bank, is as well known for its celebrity customers as its quality produce while Marché des Batignolles is an organic market with over 70 stalls.

Although markets supply the bulk of the weekly groceries, specialty food shops provide the opportunity to gaze longingly at beautifully packaged artisan products. Luxury foodstuffs are the order of the day at Fauchon food hall and also at Le Comptoir de la Gastronomie, where the finest regional specialties can be purchased. Tea lovers are advised to visit La Maison des Trois Thés to wonder at some of the most exclusive teas in the world and foie gras fans are spoilt for choice in Maison Pou. For wine, there is an endless choice of shops: Lavinia is a one-stop shop whereas La Maison des Millésimes stocks only Bordeaux and Les Grandes Caves specializes in wines from lesser-known producers.

WHERE TO EAT

• • • • • • • • • • • • • • •

✖✖✖
L'ATELIER DE JOËL ROBUCHON
5, rue de Montalembert
75007 Paris
t +33 1 42 22 56 56
w www.joel-robuchon.com

It's impossible to mention restaurants without including one of the country's most famous establishments. Diners have a more tangible experience as they watch the delicate tapas-inspired plates of food being prepared.

✖✖
CAFÉ DE LA PAIX
5, place de l'Opéra
75009 Paris
t +33 1 40 07 36 36
w www.cafedelapaix.fr

It oozes opulence and sophistication. While it might be famous it's worth a visit for the history and the chance to sample some expertly cooked classic French food.

✖
FRENCHIE
5, rue du Nil
75002 Paris
t +33 1 40 39 96 19
w www.frenchie-restaurant.com

The pared-back design and diminutive menu in this trendy establishment have helped to inject a new lease on life into French bistro dining.

Loire Valley

The mere mention of the Loire Valley conjures up images of grand châteaux, manicured gardens, world-class wines, photogenic villages and markets spilling over with ripe fruit and fragrant flowers.

WHERE TO EAT

✖✖✖

DOMAINE DES HAUTS DE LOIRE

Route de Herbault
41150 Onzain
t +33 2 54 20 72 57
w www.domaine
    hautsloire.com

This beautiful château will impress even the most well-traveled gourmand. The food is classic and top-notch and there is accommodation to match.

✖✖

BRASSERIE DE L'UNIVERS

8, place Jean Jaurès
37000 Tours
t +33 2 47 05 50 92

Typical French cooking in historic surroundings at this popular brasserie. The food is faultless and the dining room impressive.

✖

LE PETIT PATRIMOINE

58, rue Colbert
37000 Tours
t +33 2 47 66 05 81

This no-frills restaurant offers excellent value for money with its lovingly prepared traditional regional dishes.

The area is certainly one of the most important and notable culinary destinations in the country, and the abundance of exceptional food and wine is a winning combination that attracts visitors from all over the world.

Geographically, the region has been blessed with a terrain and climate that suits a multitude of agricultural uses. The fields yield a wonderful array of quality fruit, vegetables and cereal crops; the vines produce a glut of quality grapes; and the goats' milk creates some of the finest cheeses in the country.

Specialties and Local Producers

Whole books could – and indeed are – dedicated to the culinary specialties of the Loire Valley but a number of special products deserve mention. Top of the huge wine list are Sancerre, Pouilly-Fumé, Touraine and Muscadet, but while wine tends to grab the headlines, note that the region also produces a number of well-

3 things you **must not** miss

1 Loire Valley Wine Festival
This annual event in June sees local wine producers convene in the Parc des Mini-Châteaux near Amboise. This quirky location contains all 43 of the region's châteaux in miniature. *www.loirevalley tourism.com*

2 Le Tasting Room
Whether you want to taste wine for an hour or a few days, this company offers a huge range of options for everyone from novice to wine buff. *www.letastingroom.com*

▶ **3 Saut-aux-Loups Mushroom Gallery**
Take a break from wine and head underground to this labyrinth of caves where various varieties of mushrooms are grown and harvested. *www.troglo-sautauxloups.com*

known liqueurs, including Cointreau and Chambord. In addition, the Loire is known for a number of classic recipes. Rich *beurre blanc* sauce, deliciously sweet and sticky *tarte tatin*, the white asparagus of the fertile Loire riverbank and slow-cooked, potted pork (*rillons*) are all synonymous with this lush valley. The area is also notable for the number of cheeses that have been given Protected Designation of Origin status. Look out for Valençay and *crottin de Chavignol*, which is without doubt the most famous goats' cheese produced in a region of fine cheeses. Port Salut is another well-known name, and it's still made to the original recipe of the Trappist monks who first produced it in 1816.

Markets and Shops
The markets of the Loire Valley are famous for their color, atmosphere and the sheer abundance of attractive offerings. Every city, town and village provides fresh fruit, meat and other produce for its residents and visitors, and there's always a market nearby. The weekly market at Amboise offers the chance to shop and marvel at the beautiful surroundings in the shadow of Château d'Amboise. Tours, Blois and Nantes are just some of the other towns with notable weekly farmers' markets. Incidentally, don't leave Amboise without visiting the delectable Pâtisserie Bigot to stock up on cakes and pastries and have a coffee. Boucherie Rubens in Nantes is a food and wine lover's enclave while in Vouvray meat is the order of the day. La Maison Hardouin has been selling top-quality rillettes, hams and terrines for over 100 years.

OPPOSITE ABOVE Port Salut is just one of the many great cheeses produced in this region.

OPPOSITE BELOW There are stunning châteaux, such as Chenonceau, around every turn in the road.

LEFT Valençay cheese is a famous product of the Loire Valley.

Lyon

The third-largest city in the country has carved out an architectural and culinary niche for itself.

ABOVE *Beaujolais is imbibed with every meal in Lyon. The grapes are grown in the Beaujolais region to the north of the city.*

OPPOSITE *Locals fill up the tables at one of Lyon's* bouchons, *where good food is served simply.*

It sneaks ahead of the competition thanks to its special location in the Rhône-Alpes with the Rhône and Saône rivers converging just outside the city center. Lyon has long been widely viewed as the food capital of the country and, although Parisians would be quick to disagree, it certainly has one hand on the gourmet crown. Furthermore, Lyon sits between two of the greatest wine regions in France, the Côtes du Rhône and Beaujolais.

Specialties and Local Producers

Lyon is bursting at the seams with top-quality local produce and specialties. As with most cities and regions in France, there is a distinctive meat product that keeps local pride running high and in Lyon it is the *andouillette*. This pork sausage is characterized by its rich, earthy, smoky flavor and proof of its local importance can be found in the Lyon fan club that rates restaurants solely on the quality of their

andouillettes. Tradition has played an important role in the success of Lyon as a food destination and, although contemporary chefs have created a buzz in the city, there remains a great deal of respect for the past. Lyon is still well known for its intimate, no-frills eateries called *bouchons*, which are unique to the area and serve simple, home-cooked fare made from local ingredients.

The location of the city between two vast Appellation d'Origine Contrôlée wine regions means that quality wine is in abundance. Good Beaujolais isn't held back for special occasions but is brought out for every meal. This includes the typical *mâchons*, a hearty morning meal of mixed charcuterie washed down with tumblers of the red wine.

Markets and Shops

You don't have to wander too far around the streets of Lyon before encountering the

3 things you **must not** miss

◀ **1 Bocuse d'Or**
This internationally celebrated chef championship aims to discover the best cooks in the business. *www.bocuse dor.com*

2 La Semaine du Goût
There are tastings, food courses and demonstrations at this weeklong October food fair. *www.legout.com*

3 Beaujolais Nouveau Festival
Join in as Lyon celebrates the release of Beaujolais Nouveau on the third Thursday of November in this festival fondly known as Beaujolympics. *www.en.lyon-france.com*

● ● ● ● ● ● ● ● ● ● ● ●

✖✖✖

L'AUBERGE DU PONT DE COLLONGES

40, rue de la Plage
69660 Collonges au
   Mont d'Or
t +33 4 72 42 90 90
w www.bocuse.fr

Don't miss the culinary greatness of Paul Bocuse. This bistro on the outskirts of the city has earned its chef three Michelin stars.

✖✖

LÉON DE LYON

1, rue Pléney – angle rue
   du Plâtre
69001 Lyon
t +33 4 72 10 11 12
w www.bistrotsde
   cuisiniers.com

Arguably the best place to sample classic French cooking in the city, accompanied by a carefully selected, extensive wine list.

✖

BRASSERIE GEORGES

30, cours de Verdun
69002 Lyon
t +33 4 72 56 54 54
w www.brasserie
   georges.com

As the oldest brasserie in Lyon, this is a popular haunt but its history and the consistency of its food make it well worth a dinner reservation. Classic Lyonnaise cuisine can be enjoyed alongside other regional dishes, in elegant surroundings.

name Paul Bocuse. This French legend revolutionized cooking in the country by popularizing the concept of nouvelle cuisine in the 1970s. His restaurants and bistros use top-quality local ingredients, many of which can be bought in the market that bears his name. Halles de Lyon–Paul Bocuse is the main market in the city and is the place to get a feel for the enormous variety and quality of foodstuffs available here.

Lyon is also known for its numerous specialty shops that offer a wide selection of the best local produce and ingredients. Sève produces chocolates and desserts that almost look too beautiful to eat. C. Reynon will introduce you to some of the charcuterie for which Lyon is so famous and Fromagerie Richard is a cheese-lover's delight, where a mother and daughter team mature their cheeses, including the celebrated local Saint-Marcellin.

Provence

This idyllic location occupies the southeast corner of the country. The stunning scenery and idealized lifestyle have made this a dream destination for foreigners yearning to start afresh.

ABOVE The vibrant colors of the fresh produce make for striking displays in the markets.

RIGHT Provence is famous for its lavender and the fields stretch away into the distance.

OPPOSITE Carpentras market is one of the best and busiest in the region, with hundreds of stalls lining the streets.

And why not? Provence ticks all the boxes in terms of climate, scenery, laid-back attitude and bountiful produce for those contemplating life abroad. Produce is often pulled from the ground and put in the pot the same day, and the concept of food miles is completely alien to the locals because markets provide the mainstay of the larder. Consumers are able to buy their food directly from the person who has grown or produced it.

Specialties and Local Producers

The Mediterranean location provides a diet with an abundance of olive oil, herbs and luscious fresh fruit. Provençal markets are full of locally grown apricots, melons, nectarines and strawberries, and fragrant sachets of herbes de Provence are one of the most familiar sights in the region. Typical dishes include *pissaladière* (Provençal pizza) and *pan bagnat*, a takeaway version of Niçoise salad, with all the ingredients neatly

3 things you **must not** miss

◀ 1 Les Baux de Provence Wine Festival
Travel to one of the most beautiful villages in France to indulge in the best regional wine and food during this May festival. *www.lesbauxde provence.com*

2 Olive Oil Tasting
Take time off from tasting wine and let your taste buds explore the variety and quality of Provençal olive oils. *www.moulin-huile-jullien.com*

3 Avignon Truffle Festival
Regional chefs gather in Les Halles market in February to get creative with this enigmatic ingredient. *www.provenceconfidential. com/en/tours-a-things-to-do-15/197-avignon-truffle-festival*

sandwiched into the center of a crusty white roll. The classic fish soup *bouillabaisse* is from Provence, as is *mesclun*, a simple mixed-leaf salad that accompanies main dishes. A number of dips and pastes are also Provence creations. *Anchoïade* is a punchy paste of anchovies, garlic and olives that can be used as a dip, sandwich filler and sauce while *pistou* and *aïoli* liven up soups and salads.

Châteauneuf-du-Pape is probably the most famous wine of the region. It hails from the village of the same name and the surrounding area. However, pastis is the drink most likely to be sipped in the bars and cafes of villages. This aniseed-flavored Provençal aperitif is the top choice when reading the paper or putting the world to rights.

Markets and Shops

It is almost meaningless to mention farmers' markets in Provence because they are as numerous as the villages. However, some are well worth a detour and they include the Friday market in Carpentras where there's an overwhelming choice with hundreds of stalls lining the streets of this delightful town. The market in Uzès is held on Saturdays and you'll get a huge taste of the culture and cuisine of Provence. Truffle lovers should head to La Maison de la Truffe where the introverted fungus is on full display with all the paraphernalia needed to prepare and cook it. Wine to accompany the truffles can be purchased from Du Chai d'Uzès or Le Ballon Rouge, which also hosts wine-tasting events.

Gourmands often make a beeline for the town of Aix-en-Provence. Pâtisserie Weibel bakes the best cakes and pastries, Le Passage Vert is a specialist organic shop and Confiserie du Roy René is well worth visiting for its confectionery. From the main thoroughfares to the narrow lanes and passageways, Aix is a wonderland of food stalls, shops and emporia.

Pork with prunes

Porc aux pruneaux
TOURS

serves **4**

1 lb 10 oz (750 g) pork tenderloin,
  cut into large chunks
Flour, for dusting
3 Tbsp olive oil
1 onion, finely chopped
2 garlic cloves, finely chopped
5 fl oz (150 ml) white wine
10 fl oz (300 ml) chicken stock
1 bay leaf
2 thyme sprigs
5 fl oz (150 ml) heavy cream
Salt and freshly ground black pepper
16 pitted prunes, 8 cut in half
½ apple, peeled, cored and chopped
Mashed potatoes, to serve

Dust the pork all over in flour. Heat 2 tbsp of the oil
in a casserole dish that is suitable for use on your
stovetop. Brown the pork all over for about 5 minutes
and then remove to a plate.

Heat the remaining oil and gently fry the onion and garlic
in the dish for 3 minutes. Return the pork to the dish
and then add the wine, stock, bay, thyme and half the
cream and season well with salt and pepper. Stir well to
combine, just bring to the boil and reduce to a very
gentle simmer and cook for 1 hour.

Add the prunes and chopped apple and a little
more stock or water, if required. Cook for a further
20 minutes then stir in the remaining cream. Serve
with mashed potatoes.

Herb omelette

Omelette aux fines herbes
FRENCH CLASSIC

serves **1**

3 large eggs
Salt and freshly ground black pepper
1 tsp each finely chopped chives, parsley
  and chervil
2 small tarragon leaves, finely chopped
2 Tbsp (25 g) unsalted butter

Beat the eggs together in a bowl and season
generously with salt and pepper. Add the herbs to the
eggs and mix again.

Heat the butter in a small nonstick pan until hot,
turning to coat the pan. Pour the egg mixture into the
pan and stir quickly for a couple of seconds to break
up the mixture.

Cook for about 2 minutes then gently tilt the pan to
fold one-third of the omelette into the centre. Repeat
with the other side so that you have a neat roll and
then carefully flip the omelette on to a plate to conceal
the join. Serve immediately.

ITALY

ALMOST EVERYONE, EVERYWHERE, is familiar with Italian food. Pizza has become *the* fast food while pasta can suit the palates and pockets of all, from struggling students to well-heeled gourmands. However, while Italian cuisine tends to be taken as a whole and its culinary exports are viewed without regard to the region in which they were produced, once you arrive in Italy you soon realize that the food is very regionalized. In the north of the country polenta and rice are far more common than pasta and you will also find some of the best risotto in Italy. And while olive oil is produced in great quantity and quality, butter is preferred in some areas, especially in the Lombardy region.

Moving south, fish and seafood become a more conspicuous part of the diet, as the Mediterranean offers a ready supply of raw ingredients. Pasta also plays a bigger part on the dinner table with regions such as Emilia-Romagna giving the country some of its most famous pastas and sauces. Tuscany shows how simple peasant food can taste incredible, Campania is a treasure trove of lush fruit and vegetables while Sicily has used its history of invasion and occupation to create a cuisine unique to Italy, rich in exotic fruits and spices.

travel essentials

TIME ZONE: GMT +1
TELEPHONE CODE: +39
CURRENCY: Euro
CAPITAL: Rome
LANGUAGE: Italian

GETTING THERE: Italy has a national airline – Alitalia – and a number of airports around the country served by regular international flights. There is also a comprehensive rail network with many international services to France, Germany, Croatia, Spain, etc. The borders with France, Switzerland, Austria and Slovenia are open, which makes arriving by car fast and efficient.

Piedmont

Piedmont might trail behind some of the better-known Italian regions in terms of tourism but its food is top quality.

ABOVE Barolo is one of the best-known names when it comes to Piedmont wine.

RIGHT Gorgonzola cheese has traveled around the world to become a favorite with cooks everywhere.

OPPOSITE A Barolo vineyard in a stunning location is a wine lover's delight.

This northern region, which is hugged by the Alps and whose name means "foot of the mountain," enjoys a wonderfully diverse cuisine that both links it to, and differentiates it from, the rest of the country. From the rice fields of lowland Piedmont to the extensive vineyards of the south, and from the orchards to the truffle-rich forests, there is a glut of gastronomic pleasures. The ingredients are fresh and exciting, the meals are lovingly prepared from recipes handed down through the generations and the locals are quick to celebrate their regional specialties.

Specialties and Local Producers

Piedmont is home to so many of Italy's great foods that it is difficult to decide where to begin. Intoxicating truffles are scarce and highly prized. Alba and Asti are the main areas for truffle hunting in Piedmont, where specially trained pigs or dogs sniff out the precious fungi. Other pigs

3 things you **must not** miss

◀ 1 Alba Truffle Festival
Get caught up in truffle fever at this October celebration of the great fungus. *www.regione.piemonte. it/turismo/*

2 Barolo Wine Tour
Drive yourself or join a tour and leave the car at the hotel. Whatever you do, don't miss the chance to visit some of the great wineries of the region. *www.italyandwine. net/piedmont/barolo.htm*

3 Gorgonzola Factory Tour
Find out how this great blue cheese is made during a visit to one of the many factories in the region. A number of tour companies offer visits, including *www.tour piedmont.com*

are reared for their quality meat and, in Piedmont, they are likely to become one of the local specialties, such as *mortadella* sausage or the famous *prosciutto*.

Piedmont is also home to a number of other iconic ingredients that have found their way into kitchens around the world. Gorgonzola is a quality blue cheese that has been accorded Protected Designation of Origin status and Arborio rice is a "must" when making risotto (see page 52). The region is equally famed for its wines, with Barolo and Barbaresco two of the best-known names. The grapes are also used to make another local beverage, grappa.

Markets and Shops

Piedmont is serious both about its food and maintaining traditional production techniques and the regional cuisine. This is aptly demonstrated by the Slow Food Movement, which began in Italy and has its

headquarters in Bra, a town in Piedmont famous for its cheese. Cascina del Cornale is a farming cooperative that reiterates the principles of Slow Food with its collective of local producers. Their products are available to buy or try in the smart shop and restaurant complex in Magliano Alfieri. Eataly is a similar enterprise with a smaller number of producers committed to growing and making top-quality food. The Eataly food and wine centre in Turin is a gastronome's haven with wine tastings, food courses and educational facilities all on one site.

There are also plenty of other opportunities to buy direct from farmers and producers in markets around the region. Alba, Bra and Asti have wonderful markets, with rich pickings if you love the local food; visitors are never more than a village or town away from the best that the local area has to offer.

WHERE TO EAT

COMBAL.ZERO
Castello di Rivoli Museo
   d'Arte Contemporanea
Piazzale Mafalda di Savoia
10098 Rivoli
t +39 011 956 5225
w www.combal.org

Treat your taste buds to the culinary creativity of head chef Davide Scabin. Italian cuisine is pushed to its limits with an array of eclectic and surprising dishes.

RISTORANTE LA CAPANNINA
Via Donati, 1
10121 Torino
t +39 011 54 5405
w www.lacapannina
   torino.com

For a true taste of Piedmontese cuisine, head straight for this lovely restaurant in the center of Turin.

RISTORANTE PINOCCHIO
Via Matteotti, 147
28021 Borgomanero
t +39 03 228 2273
w www.ristorante
   pinocchio.it

Take a culinary tour around Piedmont at this elegant family eatery. The best ingredients are used to create simple regional dishes with a contemporary flavor.

The two ancient regions of Emilia and Romagna were combined to form this one large region in the north of the country, which is a glorious geographical mix of mountains, plains and coastline.

WHERE TO EAT

☼☼☼

OSTERIA FRANCESCANA

Via Stella, 22

41100 Modena

t +39 059 210 118

w www.osteria
francescana.it

This smart dinner venue is the place for cutting-edge Italian cuisine.

☼☼

RISTORANTE DIANA

Via Indipendenza, 24

40121 Bologna

t +39 051 231 302

w www.ristorante
dianabologna.com

Head to this elegant restaurant for a taste of authentic Bolognese cuisine.

☼

TRATTORIA DA PIETRO

Via de' Falegnami, 18/A

40121 Bologna

t +39 051 648 6240

w www.trattoriadapietro.it

This is hard to beat for authentic, rustic dining. The specialty is fresh, handmade pasta, with plenty of meat to follow.

The capital, Bologna, marks the historic border between Emilia to the west and Romagna to the east. The region's substantial culinary gift to Italy is agriculture (a major part of the local economy) and the endless rows of vines in Romagna that help boost Italy's wine industry.

Pasta is the carbohydrate of choice in Emilia-Romagna and some of the most well-traveled pasta recipes originated here. The region is characterized by its honest, satisfying food that delivers on flavor and relies on the quality of its ingredients.

Specialties and Local Producers

Emilia-Romagna is a treasure trove of ingredients that have reached a lofty status among food aficionados the world over. Parmigiano-Reggiano can only be produced in a few areas of Italy in order to be credited with this name and Emilia-Romagna is one of them. This hard, flavorful cow's-milk cheese is a "must buy" around the world.

Parma is famous for its *prosciutto*, which is also a product that is protected by the EU. The best way to savor its special

flavor is to eat it on its own. Just down the road in Modena, balsamic vinegar has been produced since the Middle Ages and this distinctive condiment is sipped and tasted like fine wine.

Another short trip east brings you to Bologna where the *mortadella* sausage was first made. The city is also famous for its handmade pasta and, in particular, *tortellini*. These tiny stuffed pasta shapes are a labor of love as their creation is time consuming and arduous. *Ragù* is a common accompaniment for *tagliatelle*, or egg noodles, and this rugged sauce of hand-chopped and slow-cooked meat sums up the hearty and wholesome cuisine of the region.

Markets and Shops

The markets in Emilia-Romagna are a colorful display of the best produce and ingredients of the region. Delicate Emilian asparagus, sun-ripened fruit, vibrant vegetables, ripe cheeses and intense wines all vie for prime position among the crowded stalls.

The Mercato di Mezze in Bologna is a feast for the eyes. This glorious food market is a rabbit warren of stalls and specialist shops, and seems to go on forever. From fresh pasta to cured hams and freshly

harvested plums and apricots, the temptations are huge. The open-air market in Parma is another colorful celebration of every kind of food. It's the ideal place to buy tasty picnic provisions.

Back in Bologna, the food shopping doesn't end when the stallholders pack up their wares. The most exquisite fresh pasta, bread and cakes can be purchased at Paolo Atti & Figli. For the more adventurous carnivore, Macelleria Equina sells horsemeat and you will find everything from sausages to pâté.

ABOVE The Mercato di Mezze in Bologna is a wonderful day out in itself.

OPPOSITE ABOVE Balsamic vinegar is a specialty of the region and a respected ingredient.

OPPOSITE BELOW The rural lifestyle is still very much at the heart of food production in Emilia-Romagna.

3 things you **must not** miss

1 Voghiera Festival
Pack your breath-freshener and head to Voghiera in August for this annual event. Garlic is king here and there are lots of opportunities to sample these prized bulbs. *www.deliciousitaly.com/prodo tto.php?id=251&regione_id=5*

2 Feast of the Cherry Trees ▶
This is one of hundreds of festivals celebrating specific ingredients. The town of Vignola comes alive during this fair in April.

3 Ferdinando Cavalli Tour and Tasting
Ferdinando Cavalli makes fine balsamic vinegar. Sample it for yourself and discover more about its production and aging. *www.balsamico cavalli.it*

Tuscany

Tuscany is the Italy of road movies with its undulating landscape, ancient towns perched precariously on hilltops and palatial estates bordered by neat clusters of cypress trees.

ABOVE Tuscan bread can be used to create a number of tasty snacks.

RIGHT When you want an ice cream, head to Vivoli.

OPPOSITE The Mercato Centrale in Florence is a must-visit for food lovers.

It is a land of intoxicating beauty, with both rural and urban settlements exemplifying Italy at its best.

Located in the center of the country, Tuscany has a natural affinity with its immediate neighbors Emilia-Romagna and Umbria but it doesn't play second best to them. There is a great deal of authority on the Tuscan dinner table, which groans under the weight of the local produce. The food might be earnest and wholesome but the raw ingredients are among the best in the country. Rich game, olive oil, fresh bread, beans and exceptional wine are among the culinary highlights in this part of Italy.

3 things you **must not** miss

◀ 1 Montepulciano Open Cellars

The main town celebrates its food and wine in this gastronomic spectacular that includes tasting and cellar tours in the last weekend of May. *www.comune. montepulciano.si.it*

2 Truffle Hunting

If you want to unearth your own piece of fungal gold, what better than a truffle hunt with an expert? *www.assotartufi.it*

3 Sassofortino Chestnut Festival

Visit different cellars combining good wine and snacks of freshly roasted chestnuts. *www.festadella castagna.info*

Specialties and Local Producers

In Tuscany the food on the table is very much linked to its place of origin. There are relatively few steps involved from harvesting vegetables or hunting game to settling down to the finished dish. The lightest of touches is used to transform raw ingredients into meals but the flavors still sing on the palate. As with all regions of Italy, Tuscany has its specialty hams: here, it is the EU-protected *prosciutto Toscano*, which is a dry-cured ham that takes on the flavors of its garlic and rosemary rub. Hearty peasant food is another culinary highlight and Tuscan bread (*pane Toscano*) is present at every meal. The dense, unsalted loaves are an acquired taste but add some olive oil and garlic and the bread is transformed into the Tuscan specialty *fettunta*. A few more added ingredients and, hey presto, it's *crostini*. The intense Pecorino Toscano cheese is also a big favorite while Tuscan olive oil is used for cooking and dressing food.

Although Tuscans are affectionately known as "bean eaters" in Italy because of their fondness for, and huge consumption of, white beans, pasta is also enjoyed, particularly when paired with rich, gamey sauces. *Pappardelle* is the Tuscan contribution to the pasta cupboard and these large, flat egg noodles are perfectly suited to the robust flavours that are piled on top of them. It is therefore no surprise that the wines of the region are typified by bold flavors to hold their own with the food, with Chianti and Montepulciano among the better-known regional wines.

Markets and Shops

There are many great towns and cities in the region, all with their share of unique shops. Florence is famous for its *gelaterias* and Vivoli is consistently praised for its delicious selection of Italian ice cream. In fact food, art and architecture are the backbone of Florence and the city is a cultural overload. When the sightseeing has been done, the Mercato Centrale provides everything required for the evening meal. This indoor market is arranged on two floors, and there are also stalls selling snacks and takeaway meals. The nearby town of Figline Valdarno again has a wonderful food market, as do Montepulciano, Lucca and too many others to mention.

The market town of Greve lies in the heart of Chianti country where Antica Macelleria Falorni is a centuries-old butcher's that sells regional specialties. Check out the many exceptional delis in the town, which offer a tempting array of cured hams, local cheeses and olive oils.

WHERE TO EAT

✕✕✕
LOCANDA DELL'AMOROSA
Località l'Amorosa
53048 Sinalunga (Siena)
Tuscany
t +39 0577 677 211
w www.amorosa.it

If you want to eat out in a picture-postcard setting, it's difficult to beat this intimate, stylish restaurant. The menu is created around seasonal ingredients celebrating the local cuisine.

✕✕
LA BOTTEGA DEL 30
Via Santa Caterina, 2
Villa a Sesta
53019 Castelnuovo
    Berardenga (Siena)
t +39 0577 359 226
w www.labottegadel30.it

Tuscan flavors are served in a delightful restaurant with a romantic terrace for summer dining.

✕
PANE E VINO
Piazza di Cestello 3 rosso
50124 Florence
t +39 0552 476 956
w www.ristorantepane
    evino.it

This consistently highly rated Florence restaurant offers excellent value for money with its Tuscan-themed menu that changes each day, and an impressive wine list.

Rome

In Rome there is an ancient monument around every corner and the city is so steeped in myth, fact and legend that it's easy to get swept away by the greatness of the place and overlook its food.

ABOVE Fava beans are a popular snack and are cooked in a simple way to preserve their taste.

RIGHT Some of the best restaurants can be discovered on innocuous side streets, away from the tourist hub.

OPPOSITE The city center market, Campo dei Fiori is a bustling outdoor grocery store.

However, besides the massive cultural significance that Rome has on the world stage, it is also one of the great food destinations.

Like any capital city, Rome has its fair share of standardized tourist venues, with conveyor-belt food and uninspiring menus. But a visitor doesn't have to be too intrepid to stumble upon food that will transform a sightseeing holiday into a gastronomic tour. From simple trattorias to high-end restaurants, the dining options are virtually endless and the food can be as memorable as the monuments.

Specialties and Local Producers

It is unusual to find a city that not only embraces the food of every region of the country but also maintains its own culinary identity with dishes unique to its environs. Rome has been a staunch advocate of its own cuisine from time immemorial, and the best way to sample the hearty local *cucina*

3 things you **must not** miss

◀ **1 National Pasta Museum**
Improve your pasta knowledge at this museum dedicated to one of the great foods of Italy. Demonstrations and workshops. *www.museo dellapasta.it*

2 Festa de' Noantri
This July festival takes over the streets of Trastevere with music, food stalls and entertainment. *www.festade noantri.it*

3 Culinary Walking Tour
Discover the secrets of the city and learn the local knowledge with a guided tour including the best cafes and lunch venues. *www.asthe romansdo.com*

Romana is to shy away from larger restaurants and head instead to one of the many osterie and trattorias, tucked away in the city's side streets. Here you can enjoy dishes featuring offal, fresh vegetables and rustic recipes, such as carbonara and gnocchi alla Romana.

Fava beans are a Roman specialty and are eaten simply with freshly grated Pecorino cheese during May. The hearty pork roast known as porchetta originated in Rome and remains popular today, as does salt cod, or baccalà, which originated in the Jewish quarter of the city. Saltimbocca alla Romana (see page 52) is a classic Roman dish that is now eaten around the world.

Markets and Shops

Going to the food markets is part of daily life in Rome. There are plenty to choose from but Campo dei Fiori in the center of the city is a favorite with the locals. This large piazza buzzes with the sounds of commerce and gossip as the daily task of shopping merges into a social gathering. Mercato di Testaccio is a more formal affair with fishmongers, butchers and cheesemongers occupying permanent stands in the covered building.

Rome also has its fair share of fine food emporia and Gusto is high on the list. You can buy and try a huge range of food and drinks because the complex contains a restaurant, wine bar, osteria and pizzeria, as well as a cheese shop and wine shop. For more wine shopping, Trimani is highly regarded and Enoteca Costantini is the largest wine shop in the city. Aquastore is exclusively stocked with water and has brands and bottles from all over the world. If this all seems a little too healthy, make a dash to Trastevere and stock up on chocolates and sweet treats from Valzani chocolatier.

WHERE TO EAT

● ● ● ● ● ● ● ● ● ● ● ● ● ●

✖✖✖
HOSTARIA DELL'ORSO
Via dei Soldati, 25c
00186 Rome
t +39 06 6830 1192
w www.hdo.it

For a grand setting this restaurant is hard to beat. Located in a refurbished 14th-century inn, the food is under the supervision of the celebrated Italian chef Gualtiero Marchesi.

✖✖
RISTORANTE TRATTORIA
Via del Pozzo delle
   Cornacchie, 25
00186 Rome
t +39 06 6830 1427
w www.ristorantetrattoria.it

A restaurant full of surprises with a contemporary interior inside a historic building. Specializing in Sicilian food, the dishes are light, modern and highly rated.

✖
CHECCO ER CARETTIERE
Il Ristorante
Via Benedetta, 10/13
Rome
t +39 06 580 0985
w www.checcoercarettiere.it

Having been in the family for three generations, this restaurant is something of an institution in the Trastevere district. Indulge in classic Roman cooking.

Sicily

Sicily is very much a part of Italy, but its separation from the mainland allows it a degree of culinary and cultural autonomy that has helped to shape its independent character.

The history of the island teaches us a lot about its food. Having been invaded by the Greeks, Arabs and Romans – among many others – Sicily has developed its own unique cuisine, influenced by all these cultures.

The food is rich, varied and exciting. It is based on a Mediterranean diet but there are plenty of unexpected twists to keep visitors on their toes. The Sicilians are passionate about citrus fruit and the vast orange and lemon groves of Palermo seem to stretch on forever. The locals have an incurable sweet tooth, a constant craving for pasta and a burgeoning wine industry about to take the world by storm. In short, the Sicilians are food lovers living in their ideal location.

Specialties and Local Producers
The number of Sicilian foods that have been given Protected Designation of Origin status provides some indication of the sheer quality of the food. Among the many varieties of citrus fruits grown on the island, Ribera oranges have been singled out for their distinctive sweet flavor. Olive oil is another specialty of the island and Val di Mazara has Protected Designation of Origin status, as does the wonderful Pagnotta del

3 things you **must not** miss

1 Ottobrata Zafferanese
Head to the town of Zafferana Etnea in October to celebrate the best local produce to the accompaniment of music and general merrymaking. *www.ottobratazafferanese.net*

2 Mandranova Olive Oil Estate
Taste some of the best olive oil in Sicily at this stunning estate where guests can also stay in the superbly renovated farmhouse. *www.mandranova.it*

▶ 3 Chocobarocco in Modica
Modica is famous for its chocolate. This annual celebration of chocolate gives visitors an insight into the magical transformation from bean to bar. *www.choco barocco.it*

Dittaino bread. This is perfect for dipping in the unctuous oil or serving with one of the local dishes, such as steamed mussels (*cozze alla marinara*) or the classic vegetable dish, *caponata*.

The huge variety of plants grown around the island has resulted in another specialty: honey. Bees feast on the nectar to produce a range of scented honeys that are enjoyed as nature intended or are used in recipes, including the wonderfully sweet Sicilian nougat called *torrone*. Sometimes, a small glass of chilled wine is the perfect accompaniment to a sweet dish or biscuit and, although Sicily is becoming better known for its wine, Marsala is the name that everyone associates with the island. This fortified wine has been produced in the town of the same name since the 18th century and is usually served as an aperitif or a dessert wine.

Markets and Shops

If Marsala is on the shopping list, a visit to Enoteca Picone in Palermo is essential. The shop stocks an extensive selection of Sicilian and Italian wines and holds regular tastings. Palermo is also home to numerous food markets. The biggest and best known is La Vucciria, and it is easy to become oblivious to time and place as you wander through the mazelike streets. Stalls are crammed with produce from land (look out for the spices and exotic vegetables) and sea. Ballarò is another food market with an overwhelming choice of foods while Catania is famous for its incredible fish market. Its displays often resemble works of modern art, with the catch of the day arranged to show off its beauty. Strolling around the market in the early morning is a crash course in seafood education.

OPPOSITE ABOVE Marsala is synonymous with Sicily.

OPPOSITE BELOW Observing the vast and varied skyline of Palermo offers a rare escape from the hustle and bustle in the streets below.

BELOW The stalls in Catania Market are laden with intricate displays of the freshest fish and seafood.

Asparagus risotto

Risotto agli asparagi
NORTHERN ITALY

serves **4**

2 Tbsp olive oil

4 Tbsp (50 g) butter

1 medium onion, finely chopped

3 ½ cups (1 L) chicken or vegetable stock

11 oz (300 g) Arborio rice

5fl oz (125 ml) white wine

14 oz (400 g) asparagus, woody stalks
   removed, and cut into ¾ in (2 cm) pieces

Salt and freshly ground black pepper

2 oz (50 g) grated Parmigiano-Reggiano
   cheese

Heat the olive oil and half the butter in a large, shallow pan. Fry the onion over medium heat, until softened.

Pour the stock into a small saucepan and place it over medium heat. Add the rice to the onion and stir well to coat it in the butter and oil. Cook for a minute until the rice grains are translucent. Pour in the wine and stir well until it has been absorbed by the rice.

Add the asparagus to the rice and season with salt. Using a ladle, gradually add the stock to the rice. After each ladle of stock has been added, gently and continuously stir the rice until it has absorbed the liquid. Continue until all the stock has been used and the rice is tender and has a creamy consistency. This will take about 20–25 minutes.

Season. Stir in the remaining butter and half the cheese, stir well, cover and set aside for 2 minutes.

Sprinkle over the remaining cheese and serve immediately.

Saltimbocca Roman-style

Saltimbocca alla Romana
ROME

serves **4**

4 x 5 oz (150 g) veal cutlets

Salt and freshly ground black pepper

4 fresh sage leaves

4 slices prosciutto

Flour, for dusting

1 Tbsp (15 g) butter

1 Tbsp olive oil

4 ½ cups (100 ml) Marsala wine

Place each veal cutlet between two sheets of plastic wrap. Roll them out to a thickness of about ¼in (5mm). Season lightly with salt and pepper.

Place a sage leaf on top of each cutlet, and then place a piece of prosciutto on top of each one. Dust the veal with flour.

Heat the butter and olive oil in a large frying pan. Fry the cutlets for about 2–3 minutes on each side, until they are cooked through. Remove from the heat and keep warm.

Add the Marsala to the pan and increase the heat to a simmer. Stir around the pan to combine the wine with all the cooking juices. Reduce the sauce for a couple of minutes and serve with the cutlets.

BELGIUM

BELGIUM IS SMALL in size but it has a big influence. As a founding member of the EU, it's at the heart of the continent's political scene and is well placed – both politically and geographically – to influence the dynamics and fortunes of the member states.

Given its numerous neighbors Belgium has had the opportunity to develop close ties with specific countries, while incorporating some of their cultural nuances into its own identity. To an extent this has included food and, as you travel around the country, it is easy to see the overlap with the Netherlands, Germany, Luxembourg and France, particularly as you reach the borders. With so much shared history, it's impossible to maintain a completely indigenous cuisine but this amalgamation of flavors and dishes, and the reinvention of certain recipes to give a specific Belgian twist, is what makes the food here so exciting.

Belgium has developed the knack of perfecting certain foods. Things are kept relatively simple but they are executed so well that the specialties of the country are widely known around Europe. Mention mussels and Belgium immediately springs to mind; the same applies to beer. The country plays to its strengths, much to the appreciation of discerning food lovers.

travel essentials

TIME ZONE: **GMT +1**

TELEPHONE CODE: **+32**

CURRENCY: **Euro**

CAPITAL: **Brussels**

LANGUAGE: **Flemish, French and German**

GETTING THERE: The main airport is Brussels, although Charleroi, which is about 25 miles (40 km) outside the city, also offers international flights. There are also a number of local airports with more limited flights. Brussels has an international train station and services operate to and from the UK, France, Germany and Switzerland. Times and frequency vary but this is definitely a viable way to travel.

Brussels

The capital of Belgium is also the unofficial capital of the EU and its importance in European politics has had a massive impact on the financial, structural and cultural make-up of the city in recent years.

ABOVE Wittamer is one of many renowned chocolatiers in Brussels.

OPPOSITE ABOVE Moules frites is the classic Belgian dish that demonstrates the quality and simplicity of the food on offer.

OPPOSITE BELOW Beer Planet is a haven for anyone with an interest in, unsurprisingly, beer.

Brussels has always had a fine culinary tradition with many specialties and a cuisine that takes its influences from its Dutch and French origins. However, there is definitely an international feel to the city with its influx of politicians and EU staff, and this is reflected in the food.

Dining out is a constant source of pleasure in Brussels. Restaurants serve good-quality local fare, knowledgeable waiters treat their job as a vocation rather than a passing phase and food is treated with the perfect combination of respect and enjoyment. Fine dining abounds but the best meals are usually enjoyed in tucked-away cafés and bistros where the beer menus read like novels and the food is cooked with flair.

Specialties and Local Producers

Brussels is famous for beer, chocolate and mussels, and visitors will have plenty of opportunities to sample all three. *Moules frites* (mussels and French fries) is the classic dish with the sturdy fried potatoes said to be a Belgian invention. Brussels waffles are another specialty not to be missed. They are readily available from street vendors and are served warm as a snack, perfect for keeping hunger pangs at bay between breakfast and lunch.

The range of locally produced beers in Brussels is staggering. The production and consumption of beer is taken very seriously but the novice can easily be overwhelmed by the selection offered in most bars and cafes. There is often a special beer menu and almost always a specific glass for each kind of beer. With beer having been produced in the country since the Middle Ages, the Belgians have got it down to a fine art and the spectrum of flavors, styles, colors and alcohol content is impressive. Cantillon is one of the best-known breweries in the city with a wide range of beers, including Kriek and Fou' Foune.

3 things you must not miss

◀ 1 Belgian Beer Weekend Festival
Keep the first weekend of September free for some serious beer tasting in the Market Place. *www.weekend delabiere.be*

2 Planète Chocolat Tour
Tour the chocolate museum and learn how to make authentic praline chocolates on this cocoa-themed excursion. *www.planete chocolat.be*

3 Walking Tour
Take a leisurely stroll around the highlights of the city and sample some of the best beer, chocolate and food that Brussels has to offer. You can opt for a self-guided tour or go with an agency. *www.itineraires.be*

Lambic beer is made using a special fermentation process and is only produced in, or very close to, Brussels.

Markets and Shops

With its reputation as one of the great chocolate-producing countries of the world, there is no shortage of places to sample and buy. Quality chocolatiers are dotted around the city and include Mary, Chocolatier Manon, Wittamer Chocolatier and Neuhaus, the company responsible for creating the praline chocolate in the early 1900s. If chocolate doesn't satisfy your sugar cravings then a visit to Biscuiterie Dandoy certainly will. The famous bakery has been preparing specialty biscuits, breads and macaroons for almost 200 years and has a number of retail outlets in the city.

If you like beer, Brussels is a paradise. Beer Planet has one of the widest selections of Belgian beer in the city and Bier Tempel will also leave you spoiled for choice while the Mandala Organic Growers market will provide the makings of a hangover cure. This group of European organic producers has its headquarters in Brussels.

WHERE TO EAT

✪✪✪ ☒
COMME CHEZ SOI
23 place Rouppe
1000 Brussels
t +32 2 512 29 21
w www.commechezsoi.be

The sumptuous art nouveau interior of this splendid building lets you know you are in for something special. The food is spectacular and tables are understandably hard to book.

✪✪ ☒
LA MAISON DU CYGNE
2 rue Charles Buls
1000 Brussels
t +32 2 511 82 44
w www.lamaisonducygne.be

Dine in opulent grandeur in this 17th-century house in the heart of Brussels where the food has earned a Michelin star. A mouth-watering menu with a choice of French and Belgian cuisines.

✪ ☒
RESTO HENRI
Vlaamsesteenweg
rue de Flandre 113
1000 Brussels
t +32 2 218 00 08
w www.restohenri.be

Dine out on authentic Belgian cuisine with a contemporary splash in this popular spot with a sensible price tag.

Chicken braised in beer

Coq à la bière
BELGIAN CLASSIC

serves **4**

8 chicken thighs or legs
Salt and freshly ground black pepper
2 Tbsp plain flour
2 Tbsp olive oil
4 Tbsp (50 g) butter
2 onions, thickly sliced
1 garlic clove, crushed
4 carrots, thickly sliced
4 celery sticks, thinly sliced
10 fl oz (300 ml) Belgian beer
2 Tbsp (25 ml) half and half

Place the chicken pieces in a large bowl and season well with salt and pepper. Dredge with flour so that the chicken is coated all over.

Heat the oil and butter in a large casserole dish that is safe for use on your stovetop, add the chicken pieces and cook over a medium heat for about 5 minutes, until they are browned. Remove from the dish and set aside.

Add the onions to the pan and fry over medium heat for 5 minutes, until softened. Add a little more oil, if necessary, then the garlic, carrots and celery and fry over medium heat for 5 minutes.

Pour the beer into the dish, season well and replace the chicken thighs. Bring to a gentle simmer then cover and cook for about 45 minutes, until the chicken is cooked through.

Remove the chicken with a slotted spoon to a warmed serving dish. Increase the heat and simmer the cooking liquid for about 2 minutes to reduce. Remove from the heat, stir in the cream and serve the sauce spooned over the chicken pieces.

NETHERLANDS

THE EAST OF the country borders Germany, the south abuts Belgium while the north and west are exposed to the North Sea. This close reliance on land and sea has played an important role in the development of Dutch cuisine. The agricultural industry has always been a major provider of food but fishing and animal rearing have had almost equal influence, and the result is a varied list of ingredients. With an abundance of vegetables, and fish jumping into nets with no encouragement, one would assume that people ate vast and elaborate meals but Dutch cuisine traditionally leant towards the essential rather than the luxurious. A simple meat and potato dish would have been perfectly acceptable to the majority of the population for most of the last century. Extravagance was frowned upon though things have now changed and there's an abundance of smoked fish and sausages, wonderful cheeses, meatballs, sauerkraut, pancakes and pastries.

travel essentials

TIME ZONE: **GMT +1**

TELEPHONE CODE: **+31**

CURRENCY: **Euro**

CAPITAL: **Amsterdam**

LANGUAGE: **Dutch**

GETTING THERE: Most visitors arrive in Amsterdam by air. Other international airports include Rotterdam and Eindhoven but they are used by fewer airlines. A number of high-speed trains connect the Netherlands to Germany, Belgium and France, and buses travel from a number of other countries as well, many offering budget tickets. The ferry is another option for those traveling from Belgium, Germany or the UK.

Amsterdam

Food comes somewhere down the list of priorities for many visitors to Amsterdam, but ignore the cuisine and you have missed a huge chunk of Dutch culture.

ABOVE *Gouda cheese is one of the most famous food exports of the Netherlands.*

BELOW *The stunning canals ensure a relaxed atmosphere in this low-key city.*

OPPOSITE *Cheese lovers will find it hard to leave De Kaaskamer delicatessen empty-handed.*

Amsterdam revels in the quality of its bars, cafes and restaurants, and the rest of the world is beginning to take note. Food stalls offer a range of specialty snacks while high-end restaurants embrace international flavors backed up by the best of local produce and ingredients.

The scenic cityscape belies the fact that Amsterdam is the financial heart of the Netherlands and the purr of bicycles overrides the rev of engines. This relaxed atmosphere continues when it comes to the food and yet Amsterdam can raise the bar when fine dining is required.

3 things you **must not** miss

◀ 1 Heineken Experience
This four-story attraction will inform you of every possible fact about this famous beer brand. There's history, brewing information, advertising and tasting to enjoy. *www.heineken experience.com*

2 Taste of Amsterdam
This four-day culinary festival in June showcases the talents of top local chefs. A great way to get an introduction to the food of the city. *www.tasteofamsterdam.com*

3 Wynand Fockink
Take a guided tour of one of the original Amsterdam *jenever* distilleries and see brewing in action. You can taste the results and buy your favorites. *www.wynand-fockink.nl*

Specialties and Local Producers

Amsterdam is a city crying out to be explored on foot or two wheels. With its network of canals and narrow streets, visitors risk missing a lot, especially the numerous street stalls, if they stick to the car. The stalls are the best places to sample some classic specialties, including sickly-sweet *stroopwafel*. These thin batter waffles are pasted together with thick syrup and are perfect for a quick energy boost during a day pounding the streets. Another street food staple are *patat*, the Dutch version of French fries. These are served with a choice of sauces, the most popular being mayonnaise.

The Netherlands is famous for its cheese, most notably Edam and Gouda. The town of Edam is a short distance from the capital and its cheese is on all the cafe menus in the capital. The country is also well known for its beer, especially Heineken. The original brewery is now a visitor attraction but there are other smaller companies that still produce beer in the city, including De Bekeerde Suster and Brouwerij 't IJ. For non-beer lovers, there are a number of other alcoholic drinks. *Jenever* is by far the most

popular local brew and Amsterdam used to be full of distilleries creating vats of "Dutch gin." Many of these have now been transformed into bars but Wynand Fockink continues to flourish after almost 300 years in the liqueur business.

Markets and Shops

A great place to try out Dutch beer and *jenever* is MiNiBar. This concept bar is like a supercharged, sophisticated drinks store. A key gives you access to your own chiller cabinet stocked with drinks.

De Kaaskamer delicatessen is a one-stop cheese shop with over 400 varieties to choose from, as well as complementary ingredients to turn your cheese into a tasty sandwich. BioMarkt stocks everything the health-food junkie could possibly crave, while Puccini Bomboni and Vanderdonk Fine Chocolates provide for their alter egos. Watershop will quench the thirst of the H_2O addict and the Boerenmarkt (organic farmers' market) has captured the growing interest in organic produce to become one of the most popular and busy markets in the city.

WHERE TO EAT

• • • • • • • • • • • • • • • •

RON BLAAUW
Kerkstraat 56
1191 JE Ouderkerk aan
   de Amstel
t +31 20 496 32 64
w www.ronblaauw.nl

With its emphasis on fresh vegetables and herbs throughout the menu this impressive restaurant serves high-end Dutch fare worthy of two Michelin stars. Located a few miles from the center of Amsterdam, the taxi ride is more than justified by the fantastic food.

DE KAS
Kamerlingh Onneslaan 3
1097 DE Amsterdam
t + 31 20 462 45 62
w www.restaurantdekas.nl

With a greenhouse supplying the restaurant with plenty of produce, you are guaranteed fresh ingredients. Dishes depend on what's available on the day but they are always exceptional.

BORDEWIJK
Noordermarkt 7
1015 MV Amsterdam
t +31 20 624 38 99
w www.bordewijk.nl

Bordewijk serves up fusion food in a congenial setting, which includes a terrace. The menu is innovative and the wine list extensive.

Vegetable hash

Stamppot

DUTCH CLASSIC

serves **4–6,**

as a side dish

6 large potatoes, peeled and diced

1 celery root, peeled and diced

1 Tbsp milk

4 Tbsp (50 g) butter

1 tsp mustard

Salt and freshly ground black pepper

Sausages or other meat of your choice, to serve

Bring a large pan of salted water to the boil, add the potatoes and celery root, bring back to a simmer and cook for about 15 minutes, until soft.

Drain well, add the milk and then mash until smooth. Add the butter, mustard and seasoning and stir again. Serve with sausages or other meat.

GERMANY

GERMANY HAS THE largest population in the EU. With a number of different countries lining its borders, there has inevitably been a wide range of influences from a wide range of sources throughout its history. Traditionally, much of the food in the country was regional, with ingredients and specialty dishes staying put within boundaries, though all that has now changed thanks to modern travel. Consequently, a lot of German food is now more national than regional, although many dishes are still known by their origins and certain areas are famous for specific foods.

Meat is one of the most important foods in the country, with thousands of different products available smoked, cured and marinated, in addition to the regular cuts of meat that feature in so many classic German dishes. Noodles and potatoes are the favorite source of carbohydrates, bread is a whole cuisine unto itself and desserts are lavish and decadent. Beer lovers travel from all over the world to indulge their passion for German-produced beer while there is plenty for wine connoisseurs to get excited about.

travel essentials

TIME ZONE: GMT +1

TELEPHONE CODE: +49

CURRENCY: Euro

CAPITAL: Berlin

LANGUAGE: German

GETTING THERE: Germany has a number of major international airports with routes all over the world. There are a couple of German airlines, the main one being Lufthansa, and they offer a range of destinations. As Germany shares a border with such a number of countries there are plenty of options for train travel, while ferries provide links to Sweden, Norway and Denmark.

Berlin

The capital city of Germany has undergone a huge change over the years and has evolved into one of the great tourist destinations of Europe.

ABOVE Bonbon Macherei turns sweet making into an art form with its incredible creations.

RIGHT Eisbein *is one of the great local dishes that is enjoyed by locals and tourists.*

OPPOSITE Berlin *is a vibrant city that has something for everyone, especially the food lover.*

Hedonists come for the festivals, the cultured for the arts and architecture while food lovers come for the unique cuisine.

Although few would argue that the food of Berlin is a refined or delicate affair, the traditional notion of rustic plates of steaming meat and accompaniments is beginning to be eroded by the spread of new German high-end dining. However, traditional ingredients and recipes are still the popular choice for most people. There is certainly no generational or class distinction when it comes to food: Berlin gets up and goes to work on the hearty, nutritious food that has seen it through its turbulent history.

Specialties and Local Producers

Berlin is liberally peppered with specialty producers and products that have endured the constant pressures of modernity. The emphasis is definitely on feel-good comfort food and *Eisbein* proves the point. This dish

3 things you must not miss

◄ 1 Currywurst Museum

Located in the heart of the city, this quirky museum will introduce visitors to Berlin's best-loved fast food. There's history, interaction and an insight into the ingredients of the legendary sauce.
www.currywurstmuseum.de

2 Tastings at Whisky & Cigars

With hundreds of whiskies from all over the world to choose from, this is a definite "must." The tasting bar will give you ample opportunity to try before you buy.
www.whisky-cigars.de

3 Bonbon Macherei Sweet Shop Tour

This sweet-lovers' paradise offers daily tours of the factory where you can see how these wonderful handmade confectioneries are created.
www.bonbonmacherei.de

of pickled ham hock is a staple and is usually served with sauerkraut or potatoes. The Berliner, a jam doughnut, deals with sugary cravings while *currywurst* is a Berlin favorite. A pork sausage is cut into bite-sized chunks and drenched in curry sauce providing the city with its popular, fast-food snack. It is easy to eat, making it ideal street food and the perfect way to soak up some of the alcohol at the end of the evening. Berlin is also famous for its quality beers and it would be a crying shame to abstain from sampling some of the best brews. *Berliner weisse* is a wheat beer usually served with a shot of fruit syrup. It has been brewed in the city since the 16th century, although there are only a couple of breweries left making this kind of beer today.

Markets and Shops

With so many dishes and ingredients to sample, it is no great surprise that food shopping is superlative in Berlin. Farmers' markets, such as Zionskirchplatz and Wittenbergplatz, offer the best local and regional produce, including plenty of quality fresh produce and homemade pickles and sauces. The weekly Crellemarket and Winterfeldmarkt offer more in the way of everyday essentials while the market at Kollwitzplatz sells exclusively organic fare every Thursday.

Organic food is increasing in popularity in Berlin and this isn't just reflected in the marketplace. Specialty food shops cater to those who want organic foods and include Fresh 'n' Friends, a supermarket stocked with organic and Fair Trade products. Meat has a large part to play in the Berlin kitchen and Fleischerei Obitz is a popular family-run butcher's. This highly regarded local shop makes its own sausages and carefully sources all the meat for sale. For cheese, look no further than Fuchs und Rabe. It stocks over 200 different varieties of cheese, as well as other delicious items. The adventurous might want to take a detour to the notorious Absinthe Depot, where a mind-altering array of varieties is on display.

WHERE TO EAT

VIVALDI
Schlosshotel
Brahmsstraße 10
14193 Berlin
t +49 30 895 84 0
w www.schlosshotel
   berlin.com

Enjoy the incredible splendor of the restaurant's interior and then try the range of regional dishes, which sit happily with classic French cuisine.

FLORIAN
Grolmanstraße 52
10623 Berlin
t +49 30 313 91 84
w www.restaurant-florian.de

This is the place to sample regional cuisine made with the finest fresh ingredients. Everything is homemade and the menu changes daily.

GUGELHOF
Kollwitzplatz/Ecke
   Knaackstraße 37
10435 Berlin
t +49 30 442 92 29
w www.gugelhof.de

It celebrates Alsatian cuisine with hearty meat dishes and rich, rustic fare. Service is attentive and the experience authentic.

Bavaria

Renowned throughout the country as a foodie region, Bavaria enjoys a certain culinary independence from the rest of Germany and has introduced its unique dishes to other parts of the country.

ABOVE The famous Hofbräuhaus brewery in Munich will offer a crash course in German beer.

RIGHT The unusual white sausage, Weisswurst, is a popular Bavarian specialty.

OPPOSITE The picture postcard scenery makes Bavaria a popular destination for fans of the great outdoors.

This southern region of Germany borders Austria, the Czech Republic and Switzerland, and has the great city of Munich as its capital. Although Bavaria is primarily known for its love of beer, it also has one of the great wine-producing regions, Franconia, in the north. With such diversity in its food and drink, it is hardly surprising that Bavaria garners a great deal of respect for its cuisine.

The landscape of Bavaria is lush and diverse. The River Danube flows through the region, and the Bavarian Alps provide a stunning backdrop to the vibrant green valleys and are a natural border with Austria.

Specialties and Local Producers

Bavaria is the largest state in the country, with a diverse range of foods and many local products. There are a number of Bavarian specialties that typify the entire region and *Schweinsbraten* is probably at the top of the list. This traditional roast pork

dish is particularly popular in Upper Bavaria where thick slices of the slow-cooked meat are served with the rock-hard crackling and the cooking juices. *Weisswurst*, which means "white sausage," is also synonymous with Bavaria. The breakfast and lunch delicacy is made from ground veal combined with bacon and is usually cooked and eaten soon after it is prepared. It is served simply with sweet mustard and another Bavarian favorite, the pretzel.

3 things you **must not** miss

◄ 1 Oktoberfest in Munich
Billed as the biggest festival in the world, it takes place over a two-week period leading up to the first Sunday in October. Traditional food and beer, with background music. *www.oktoberfest.de*

2 Munich Bike Tour
Various companies offer part- or full-day cycling tours of the city. A great way to acclimatize and try some of the best beer gardens in Munich. *www.mikes biketours.com*

3 Hofbräuhaus Tour
Take a tour around this Munich brewery and sample some of its famous beers. *www.hofbraeuhaus.de*

With its rolling hills and plentiful pastures, local cheese is obviously an important food. The hard *Bergkäse* is made from cows' milk and is produced during summer in the mountainous areas of the region, and the subtly flavored Bavarian smoked cheese has become popular all over the world. The list of beers produced in this region runs to hundreds, so let's differentiate the two main types. *Weissbier* is a white beer made from barley and wheat while the more widely consumed *Helles* is made from barley, hops and water.

Markets and Shops

Bavarians are avid market shoppers. Munich has an incredible number and variety of markets to choose from, including the long-established Pfanzelplatz and the daily market at Viktualienmarkt. Other notable markets in the region include the daily farmers' market held in the Hauptmarkt in Nuremberg.

Visit any town in Bavaria and the smell of fresh bread will induce morning hunger pangs. Luckily, the bakeries of the region more than live up to their reputation and provide the population with a constant supply of one of their staple foods. In Munich, Hofpfisterei is a traditional bakery with a deserved reputation for quality produce while the Fränkische Dorfbäckerei Karg is a bread and cake institution in Schwabach and the surrounding area, with its range of local specialties and national favorites. Dallmayr, in Munich, is the ideal place for a coffee and the best regional produce.

WHERE TO EAT

RESIDENZ HEINZ WINKLER
Kirchplatz 1
83229 Aschau im Chiemgau
t +49 8052 1799 0
w www.residenz-heinz-winkler.de

Germany's most famous chef provides top-quality ingredients and exacting cooking standards.

PAULANER BRÄUHAUS
Kapuzinerplatz 5
80337 Munich
Bayern
t +49 89 5446 110
w www.paulaner-brauhaus.de

Considered one of the most stunning dining locations in Munich, it combines the two great loves of food and beer. Typical Bavarian fare is served at this enormous, legendary venue.

HALALI
Schönfeldstraße 22
80539 Munich
t +49 89 285 909
w www.restaurant-halali.de

This restaurant is about as traditional as you're likely to get in the region. Big, hearty meat dishes packed with flavor are delivered by efficient staff.

Rhineland

The local wines are among the best in the world, and touring and tasting the huge variety on offer is also a glorious way to experience the landscape. But don't ignore the food.

WHERE TO EAT

✖✖✖

LE VAL D'OR

55442 Stromberg

t +49 6724 9310 0

w www.johannlafer.de

Johann Lafer is a culinary star running this restaurant in the Castle Stromburg, which has been recognized by Michelin.

✖✖

EURENER HOF

Hotel Eurener Hof

Eurenerstraße 171

D-54294 Trier

t +49 6518 2400

w www.eurener-hof.de

Rustic fare is the mainstay of the kitchen's output, although a gourmet selection offers a change of direction.

✖

**ALTE MÜHLE
THOMAS HÖRETH**

Mühlental 17

56330 Kobern-Gondorf

t +49 2607 6474

w www.alte-muehle-
    hoereth.de/

This family-run establishment offers guests a variety of home-made food that revels in its Rhineland origins.

The Rhineland is a loose name denoting that part of western Germany that hugs the River Rhine. With a border touching the Netherlands, Belgium and Luxembourg, it's a region with international points but a decidedly German feel. The area is mainly characterized by its wine and much of the land along the steep valleys is dedicated to vines.

Specialties and Local Producers

The region is studded with pockets of delectable gourmet treats. The cuisine is trimmed of unnecessary ingredients but, far from resulting in drab or austere meals, this merely makes the main components shine. Westphalian ham takes on the subtle flavor of the juniper wood over which it is smoked, and it doesn't need any fancy

garnishes to bring out the flavor. *Moselhecht* is a dish of pike served with a silky cheese sauce that proves there is more to Mosel than just its fine wine. *Reibekuchen* (see page 72) are little potato pancakes that are popular all over the region, as is *Himmel und Erde* (meaning heaven and earth), in which potatoes are mashed with apple sauce and served with onions and black pudding.

Rhineland is as proud of its beer as its wine, and the most famous regional offering is Kölsch, which is brewed in Cologne. Another favourite is *Altbier*, a traditional German ale with a deep amber color and a long history.

Markets and Shops

German markets are legendary and the Rhineland is no exception. Christmas markets pop up in every major town and city during the festive season, and the array of food and drink is quite incredible. For daily food shopping, the markets supply virtually everything you might need and the quality is consistently good.

Cologne has a number of farmers' markets, as well as specialty shops such as Käsehaus Wingenfeld where you can lose yourself in the vast array of cheeses on offer. If the mouthwatering cakes, biscuits and jams on show at Café Fromme become too much to bear, you can always sit down and devour something on the spot. Münstermann Delikatessen is a fine-food shop in Düsseldorf old town where every item on the shelves is carefully selected by the owner. If all this makes you feel sorry for your pets, a quick trip to Dog's Deli for beautifully packaged treats and nibbles will solve the problem.

ABOVE Westphalian ham is smoked over juniper to give it its unique flavor.

OPPOSITE ABOVE Many German cities and towns are famous for their Christmas markets and Cologne is no exception.

OPPOSITE BELOW The vineyards of the Mosel Valley produce some of the best wines in the country.

3 things you must not miss

1 Dürkheimer Wurstmarkt Wine Festival

This September celebration of wine is one of the biggest festivals in the German calendar. From big concerns to small producers, there's plenty to choose from while the food and entertainment add to the atmosphere. *www.duerkheimer-wurstmarkt.de*

2 Kaisertafel Food Festival

Try some of the delicacies presented by local food producers at this August festival celebrating the best in regional fare. *www.kaisertafel.com*

▶ 3 Bernkastel-Kues

This picturesque town in the wine-growing region of the Mosel Valley is a gastronomic treasure trove. It is also the location of the Middle Mosel Wine Festival in September. *www.bernkastel.de*

Lower Saxony

As the second-largest state in Germany, Lower Saxony certainly has the space to get creative with its food. It is located in the northwest of the country where the city of Hannover is its capital.

ABOVE Lower Saxony is one of the main cereal-producing areas in Germany.

RIGHT The spicy heat of the pinkel sausage is toned down with a portion of kale.

OPPOSITE Goslar hosts a popular farmers' market that specializes in the best local produce.

Lower Saxony is blessed with a diverse landscape that provides it with the means to produce food that is rich and varied. The coastline fills fishing nets with seafood, the adjoining flat grasslands support herds of cattle and the rich soil is ideal for growing cereal crops and vegetables.

The food is hale and hearty – as in many German regions – but there is more diversity here than in other areas, not least because of the ocean. Fish and seafood dishes are conspicuous and although specialty cured meats are popular there is a greater choice of vegetable dishes and a wide variety of fruit. Lower Saxony represents the best of Germany.

Specialties and Local Producers

If you like sausages and cured meats, Lower Saxony holds its own against its neighboring regions. The spicy *Pinkel* sausage is a local specialty and is usually

served with a generous portion of kale, and *Bregenwurst* is often stewed until it becomes a smooth paste.

Bockbier is the specialty beer of the region, and this dense, malty brew has a high alcohol content that can catch out first-timers. However, beer is far from being the only tipple of choice in Lower Saxony. The cereal spirit, *Korn*, comes from the

3 things you must not miss

◀ 1 Einbeck
The town of Einbeck in the center of Lower Saxony has one of the oldest breweries in the country. The place is steeped in the traditions of its brewing culture and is the ideal place to sample the local brew. www.einbeck-online.de

2 Saxony Asparagus Route
Asparagus is the king of vegetables in Lower Saxony and the Asparagus Route is a 460 mile (750km) circuit providing some of the best scenery, with many chances to see fields of green spears. www.niedersachsen-tourism.de

3 Rausch Schokolade
Immerse yourself in a world of chocolate as you take a tour around the museum, discover the mysteries of the Aztecs and watch the incredible sweet treats being created in the factory. www.rausch-schokolade.de

region but is popular all over the country and is usually drunk as a shot, although it is sometimes added to beer. If this sounds a little heavy on the palate then head to East Frisia. This is the unlikely tea capital of the country and its popularity evolved from humble beginnings because tea was the cheap drink of choice for the working classes. The preparation of the now-revered beverage has reached ceremonial proportions with a set routine for brewing and preparation.

Lower Saxony also has its fair share of other specialty foods, including the cows'-milk curd cheese called *Harzer*, which has an incredibly low fat content of around 1 per cent. And it would be criminal to omit the famous Bahlsen biscuits.

Markets and Shops

Lower Saxony has bustling farmers' markets in towns such as Goslar and Kassel that offer the best local produce, and specialties can be bought directly from the producer in many cases. If cheese is on your shopping list then don't miss the European Cheese Center in Hannover. This fascinating place is a shop-cum-museum with cheeses from all over the country, and indeed the world. If a cheese is worth tasting then it will almost certainly be here.

The Market Hall in Hannover old town is a wonderful venue for browsing and buying and you will find everything from fresh produce to regional specialties, as well as plenty of stalls for a quick lunchtime snack.

GASTWIRTSCHAFT WICHMANN
Hildesheimer Straße 230
30519 Hannover
t +49 511 831 671
w www.gastwirtschaft-wichmann.de

Enjoy hearty local fare in this picturesque setting, which is a short hop to the south of the city center. The gardens are perfect for alfresco summer dining.

LANDHAUS AMMANN
Hildesheimer Straße 185
30173 Hannover
t +49 511 830 818

A traditional restaurant serving fine uncomplicated food that eschews contemporary twists. The hearty cuisine of Lower Saxony is evident and customers can enjoy classic dishes of meat and noodles.

BREMER RATSKELLER
Am Markt
28195 Bremen
t +49 421 321 676
w www.ratskeller-bremen.de

This fascinating cellar restaurant is the place for typical fare – it has been dishing up hearty favorites for hundreds of years.

Baden-Württemberg

Baden-Württemberg is a tour de force in the German culinary world, and it has certainly worked hard to become one of the great food destinations in the country.

ABOVE White asparagus is a popular delicacy all over the region.

RIGHT Cities such as Heidelberg offer visitors the perfect combination of charm and quality when it comes to dining out.

OPPOSITE ABOVE The Black Forest isn't just famous for its cake; the ham is renowned as well.

OPPOSITE BELOW Despite the chocolate-box appearance, farms in the Black Forest are hard-working and productive.

This large state takes up the southwestern corner of Germany and borders a number of other countries, including France and Switzerland. This has undoubtedly had an influence on the culture and cuisine of the region but its diversity isn't solely linked to the bordering nations. With the magical landscape of the Black Forest, the wonderful wines of Baden and the romantic cities of Heidelberg and Freiburg, it is no wonder that this region is one of the most popular with tourists from all over Europe.

3 things you **must not** miss

◄ 1 Cannstatter Wasen Festival
This Stuttgart beer festival is second only in size to Oktoberfest. Originally a harvest festival celebration, the two-week festival in September and October is now dedicated to eating, drinking and entertainment. *www.cannstatter-volksfest.de*

2 Heilbronn Weindorf Festival
A wine festival in the heart of vine country, this is a local party that gets the whole town of Heilbronn celebrating. Taste the local wine and tuck into plenty of delicious snacks during a week of partying in September. *www.heilbronn-marketing.de*

3 Schwäbisches Brauereimuseum
Take a trip to the Stuttgart brewery museum for a fascinating insight into the history of beer making in this region with the chance to taste some beers. *www.stuttgart-tourist.de*

Specialties and Local Producers

The food of Baden-Württemberg is varied and easy to differentiate according to its area of origin. Baden is a long strip that follows the meandering River Rhine along its east bank and the cuisine of this area is based around potatoes, soups and stews, as well as the white asparagus that has gained worldwide recognition for its quality. The ancient area of Swabia in the south of the region is the home of *spätzle* noodles. They are short egg noodles that accompany meat dishes or are eaten with cheese and fried onions as a dish on their own. Swabia has also added *Flädle* to the German cookbook. These are simple pancakes cut into thin strips and added to soups for bulk. Kirsch is the local spirit with a clear appearance belying the flavor of morello cherries.

The Black Forest has been recognized as a quality culinary producer and its ham has been given Protected Designation of Origin status by the EU. The seasoned ham takes a long time to mature because it is cured with spices and then smoked to add a unique flavor. The ubiquitous 1970s dinner-party dessert, Black Forest cake, is also a regional specialty that seems to be enjoying a revival on European dinner tables.

Markets and Shops

With such a wealth of specialty foods and ingredients, you'd be right to expect the food shopping in Baden-Württemberg to be of an equally high standard. The region has more Michelin stars than any other in Germany, and food is taken extremely seriously. There is a farmers' market in Münsterplatz in Freiburg most days and the market in Heidelberg includes organic producers. Heil Feinschmeckerladen is a well-stocked delicatessen in Heidelberg specializing in organic food, Fair & Quer is a large organic supermarket and Mantei has a chain of bakeries in the city. In Stuttgart, Bäckerei Bernd Bosch and Treiber serve the freshest, tastiest loaves, Épicerie Fine is a delicatessen stocked with gourmet products and Metzger Luz is the place to go for quality meat.

WHERE TO EAT

WERNER'S RESTAURANT
Schloss Eberstein Hotel
Werner Gourmet GmbH
D-76593 Gernsbach
t +49 7224 995 9500
w www.schloss
      eberstein.com

This opulent dining room is set within a stunning castle. Fresh produce forms the basis of the simple menu of classic dishes.

TRAUBE TONBACH
Tonbachstraße 237
72270 Baiersbronn im
      Schwarzwald
t +49 7442 4920
w www.traube-tonbach.de

A luxurious hotel complex with four restaurants, each serving a different cuisine. The quality is superlative in each venue, with celebrated chef Harald Wohlfahrt at the helm in Schwarzwaldstube.

ALTE POST
Das Wein- und Seminarhotel
An der B 3
79379 Müllheim
t +49 7631 17870
w www.alte-post.net

Enjoy home-cooked food and wines from the local region at this country-style eatery. There are set menus or à la carte and the service is consistently praised.

Potato pancakes

Reibekuchen

RHINELAND

serves **6, as an accompaniment**

2 large eggs
¼ tsp nutmeg
1 medium onion, grated
Salt and freshly ground black pepper
6 medium baking potatoes, peeled
2 Tbsp flour
3 Tbsp vegetable oil

Beat the eggs in a mixing bowl, add the nutmeg
and onion and combine. Season well with salt
and pepper.

Grate the potatoes by hand, or use a food processor.
Pat dry with paper towels and then add to the onion
mixture and combine well. Season again and sprinkle
with the flour.

Heat the oil in a large frying pan, take small handfuls
of the mixture and place in the pan, shaping them
into patties.

Cook the patties for about 2–3 minutes on each side,
until they are a golden color. Drain on paper towels
then transfer to a serving plate. Repeat until all the
mixture is used, adding more oil as necessary.

Bavarian sausage salad

Bayerischer Wurstsalat

BAVARIA

serves **2, as a side dish**

1 Tbsp Dijon mustard
¼ tsp paprika
1 Tbsp capers
2 small dill pickles
3 Tbsp vinegar
2 Tbsp vegetable oil
Salt and freshly ground black pepper
½ lb (225 g) *knackwurst*, cooked, cooled and
   cut into thin strips or slices
1 medium onion, roughly chopped
1 Tbsp parsley, chopped

To make the salad dressing, combine mustard,
paprika, capers, pickles, vinegar and oil in a large
serving bowl. Season well with salt and pepper.

Add the *knackwurst* and onion to the bowl and
combine. Adjust the seasoning if necessary, sprinkle
chopped parsley on top and serve immediately.

AUSTRIA

LANDLOCKED AUSTRIA SITS in the heart of Europe and is known for its chocolate-box scenery thanks to the Alps. The mountainous landscape provides a stunning backdrop to the Alpine towns that trade on their natural good looks and ensure that the view isn't spoiled by any unsightly architecture. The country is rich in culture and has one of the highest standards of living in Europe, and close trading partnerships with its eight neighbors (Germany, Czech Republic, Slovakia, Hungary, Slovenia, Liechtenstein, Italy and Switzerland). Austria has plenty of opportunities to trade without looking too far afield.

This collection of border countries has also had a significant impact on the food in Austria. Areas close to the borders have been more affected than others, resulting in unique interpretations of classic central European dishes over the years. But Austria's very own classics have also influenced other countries' cuisines.

travel essentials

TIME ZONE: GMT +1
TELEPHONE CODE: +43
CURRENCY: Euro
CAPITAL: Vienna
LANGUAGE: German

GETTING THERE: Austria has six airports offering international flights. Bus and coach travel is popular in Austria and there are plenty of services to neighboring countries. Trains are fast and reliable and, again, offer a good choice of destinations at very regular intervals. If taking your own car, the fast motorways connect with all the border countries.

Salzburg

Perched on the edge of the western border, a stone's throw from Germany, the city of Salzburg basks in its baroque finery.

ABOVE Speck is produced in the Tyrol and its quality has ensured a worldwide status.

OPPOSITE ABOVE The streets of Salzburg are lit up for the Christmas market.

OPPOSITE BELOW Specialty coffees are served with cakes and pastries. Einspänner *is a popular choice.*

Although it is one of the better-known and oft-visited Austrian cities, it is only the fourth-largest in the country. Salzburg is famous for many things: Mozart was born here, *The Sound of Music* was partly set in the city and it's a UNESCO World Heritage Site. However, despite its beauty, renown and elegance, Salzburg goes about its daily business while visitors stand in awe. Once they have worn themselves out looking at the seemingly endless display of castles, palaces and manicured gardens, there's an excellent range of restaurants.

Specialties and Local Producers

As Salzburg practically sits on the border next to Bavaria in Germany, there is bound to be a certain level of culinary overlap between the two regions. Indeed, Salzburg has warmly embraced many of the

ingredients and traits of this famous cuisine and this is evident in the cafes and restaurants around the city. Sausages and cured ham are prominent fixtures in *Gasthaus* eateries, which specialize in good-value, local fare. Speck is an Austrian specialty ham that is produced in the Tyrol region, to the southwest of Salzburg, and its proximity to the city means that this delicate ingredient has found its way into the everyday diet.

Austrians have a particularly sweet tooth and Salzburg boasts a number of famous national desserts that often pop up on restaurant menus, notably the sweet Salzburg soufflé and the ubiquitous apple strudel. The coffee-house culture has also helped keep a love of desserts and cakes alive while encouraging people to take time out and sit down for a chat over a cup of

3 things you **must not** miss

◀ 1 Zotter Chocolate Factory Tour
If you are a cocoa-bean fiend this tour should satiate some of those cravings. As well as the chocolate factory there is a cinema and shop.
www.zotter.at

2 Mozart Concert and Dinner
It might be something of a tourist excursion but it would be hard not to be seduced by the traditional recipes served in the sumptuous baroque surroundings of the oldest restaurant in Europe. Professional musicians perform during dinner.
www.salzburg-concerts.com

3 Christmas Markets
These markets are popular all over Europe but the sheer beauty of this city makes the Salzburg markets even more magical. A great place to buy presents and souvenirs and to get into the festive spirit.
www.visit-salzburg.net

✪✪✪
MAGAZIN
Augustinergasse 13
5020 Salzburg
t +43 662 841584 0
w www.magazin.co.at

This wine bar, restaurant, bistro and cookshop is one of the hottest locations in the city. The food is as unusual and sophisticated as the building, which is cut into the mountainside.

✪✪
AUGUSTINER BRÄUSTÜBL
Augustiner Bräu Kloster
  Mülln OG
Lindhofstrasse 7
5020 Salzburg
t +43 662 431 246
w www.augustinerbier.at

The best beer garden in Salzburg was once part of a monastery. It is a popular summer destination for locals who come to enjoy food and drink on the large terrace with its huge trees providing valuable shade.

✪
GASTHAUS ZUM WILDER MANN
Getreidegasse 20
5020 Salzburg
t +43 662 841 787
w www.wildermann.co.at

If you want to sample the ultimate in traditional Austrian fare, book a table here. The interior is unashamedly rustic and low-key but the food is just about the best in town.

coffee. Some of the magnificent cafes are hundreds of years old, and the combination of history and dedication to providing the best beverages and patisserie makes the ritual of going out for coffee an important event.

Markets and Shops

Salzburg has a number of artisan chocolatiers with Café Konditorei Fürst just one of many establishments that has perfected the art of chocolate. For a healthier shopping trip, the daily Grüner Markt will ensure that the larder is well stocked with an abundance of fresh fruit, vegetables and traditional meats and cheeses, while the fish market supplies a fantastic range of seafood. The beautifully appointed Feinkost Kölbl delicatessen sells

an impressive range of gourmet products, as well as snacks and light lunches that can be eaten at the bar tables. Reichl is another highly rated delicatessen where cheese and wine can be bought with freshly baked loaves. The quirky Tea & Company shop scours the world for the finest tea leaves.

Vienna

Vienna (that's the name of both the state and the city) lies in the northeast of the country where it has almost one-quarter of the population of Austria.

WHERE TO EAT

✪✪✪

STEIRERECK

Am Heumarkt 2A/ im
Stadtpark
1030 Vienna
t +43 1 713 3168
w www.steirereck.at

*This restaurant has
survived the hype to
remain one of the best in
the city. The cheese trolley
is legendary.*

✪✪

ÖSTERREICHER IM MAK

Stubenring 5
1010 Vienna
t +43 1 714 0121
w www.osterreicher
immak.at

*This trendy restaurant in the
Museum of Applied Arts is
a popular dining spot.*

✪

CAFÉ SACHER

Philharmonikerstrasse 4
1010 Vienna
t +43 1 51 4560
w www.sacher.com

*Experience the coffee-
house tradition at the home
of the Sacher-Torte. The
opulent interior is far too
grand to be called a "cafe";
it elevates coffee and cake
to another dimension.*

The River Danube meanders through the city, with most of the cultural and architectural sights located to the east of the riverbank. Vienna is famous for its arts and cultural legacy, especially the theater and opera. The city has a number of prestigious theaters and arts venues attracting visitors in the thousands. Others travel here to marvel at some of the reasons why Vienna was given UNESCO World Heritage status in 2001. As for food, Vienna follows in the great Austrian coffee-house tradition with desserts being given pride of place. People treat themselves to guilt-free sweet indulgences because, well, life's too short.

Specialties and Local Producers

Wiener schnitzel, apple strudel and Sacher-Torte are certainly on most lists of famous Viennese offerings. *Schnitzel* is a flattened veal cutlet that is coated in breadcrumbs and fried until golden brown, and it has been served in city restaurants for hundreds of years. Dumplings are another popular Viennese specialty and, in particular, delicious little curd-cheese bites called *Topfenknödel*.

3 things you **must not** miss

1 Freistadt Brewery Tour

This unusual brewery is entirely owned by the citizens of the town and is well worth a visit. The tour takes visitors through the history, production and sampling of this famous beer.
www.freistaedter-bier.at

2 Cobenzl Winery

Cobenzl enjoys a stunning location just outside Vienna and a guided tour of the press houses and cellar can easily be incorporated into a weekend visit. You can also taste some of the award-winning wines.
www.weingutcobenzl.at

▶ 3 Vienna Festival

Although ostensibly a cultural event, this five-week festival in May and June is the highlight of the Viennese calendar and the whole city comes alive with theater, concerts and performances.
www.festwochen.at

When the main course is over, it's time to indulge in one of Vienna's celebrated desserts and apple strudel (see page 78) is a much-loved dish that keeps the coffee houses of the city busy baking a never-ending supply. Sacher-Torte, the classic layered chocolate cake that was invented by Franz Sacher in Vienna in the mid-19th century remains the classic Viennese dessert.

Both might be accompanied by a small glass of schnapps, the fruit spirit that is popular all over Central Europe and is traditionally imbibed at the end of a meal. Cider and perry are also popular alcoholic drinks in Vienna, and there are a number of cider-producing areas located in the surrounding region of Lower Austria guaranteeing good quality.

Markets and Shops

The markets of Vienna are known for their superlative quality and range of food. The Saturday farmers' market is a treasure trove of the finest produce and specialty products. Naschmarkt offers more in the way of international produce while the annual Christmas markets are among the best in Europe.

For indoor shopping, Julius Meinl in downtown Vienna should keep gourmets happy with its vast selection of condiments, coffees and other culinary goodies. There is even a tiny wine bar in the basement where you can enjoy a glass of something chilled and alcoholic. For further gastronomic pampering, head to Altmann & Kühne, where exquisitely packaged chocolates and sweets line the shelves. At Gerstner you can sample the chocolates and desserts in the cafe or buy supplies to eat later.

LEFT The upmarket delicatessen Julius Meinl houses a treasure trove of ingredients.

OPPOSITE ABOVE The Sacher-Torte was invented in the city and remains one of the most popular desserts.

OPPOSITE BELOW The stunning Staatsoper (State Opera House) is considered the number-one opera venue in Central Europe.

Apple strudel

Apfelstrudel
VIENNA

serves **4–6**

2 Tbsp granulated sugar
¼ tsp ground cinnamon
1 Tbsp all-purpose flour
2 large green eating apples
   (such as Granny Smith),
   peeled, cored and sliced
3 Tbsp raisins
Flour, for dusting
1 sheet puff pastry
1 egg, beaten
Powdered sugar, for dusting

Preheat the oven to 350°F/180°C/Gas Mark 4.

In a large bowl, mix together the sugar, cinnamon and flour. Add the apples and raisins to the bowl and stir gently to combine.

Lightly dust a clean work surface with flour. Roll out the pastry and spoon on the apple and raisin mixture, leaving a space of about 1in (2.5cm) around all the edges. Carefully roll the pastry away from you into a neat sausage shape, tucking in the edges of the pastry to keep the mixture inside. Finish with the join underneath, place the strudel on a baking sheet and brush all over with the beaten egg.

Bake in the oven for 35–40 minutes, until the pastry is a golden color. Transfer to a rack and leave until cool enough to handle. Dust with powdered sugar and serve in slices.

Ham hash

Gröstl
TYROL

serves **2–3**

1 lb (450 g) boiling potatoes, peeled
1 Tbsp vegetable oil
¾ lb (350 g) smoked bacon lardons
   (or cooked ham)
1 onion, roughly chopped
1 tsp sweet paprika
1 tsp caraway seeds
Salt and freshly ground black pepper
Small handful parsley, roughly chopped
Fried eggs, to serve

Bring a large pan of water to the boil and cook the potatoes for about 15–20 minutes. Drain and set aside, until cool enough to handle. Cut into small dice.

Heat the oil in a large frying pan, add the bacon and onion and cook for about 6–8 minutes over medium heat, until the bacon is golden. Remove to a plate, then put the potatoes in the pan and fry for 6–8 minutes, until golden.

Add the paprika and caraway seeds to the pan and season well with salt and pepper. Fry, stirring, for 1–2 minutes.

Return the bacon and onion to the pan and adjust the seasoning, if necessary. Sprinkle with parsley and serve immediately, with a fried egg on top.

CZECH REPUBLIC

A FASCINATING COUNTRY appealing to historians, nature lovers and foodies, with a diverse landscape ranging from high mountain peaks to leisurely flowing rivers and verdant valleys. The oft-visited capital city, Prague, is a massive draw for tourists with its fine baroque architecture and vast cultural cachet.

Czech food is hearty and dense. As a landlocked country, saltwater fish is hard to come by and, although some freshwater varieties are available, people prefer to eat meat, and plenty of it. Beef, lamb, pork and poultry are all popular, as is game, and all are usually coupled with a generous helping of potatoes or dumplings. Vegetables are eaten but they take a back seat with meat and carbohydrates being the main fare. This traditional cuisine has more recently been given a lighter, more sophisticated touch by some of the new city restaurants and, as elsewhere in Central Europe, the cuisine is undergoing some exciting changes.

travel essentials

TIME ZONE: **GMT +1**

TELEPHONE CODE: **+420**

CURRENCY: **Czech Crown**

CAPITAL: **Prague**

LANGUAGE: **Czech**

GETTING THERE: Although there are a number of airports around the country offering international flights, Prague is the major terminus. There are bus routes between a number of countries, including Germany, Switzerland and Austria. Visitors also come by train from neighboring countries. Trains within the country are reliable and reach many of the more remote parts of the country.

Prague

Although Prague sits more or less in the middle of the Czech Republic and benefits from having easy access to the regional cuisines of the entire country, it still retains its own specialties.

ABOVE Kozel's Medium is a popular beer that is brewed locally and served in bars all over the city.

RIGHT An overhead view of the old town offers a new perspective on Prague.

OPPOSITE Havelská Market is a one-stop grocery shop and a great way to get a feel of the city.

The food is filling but the health conscious might be hard-pressed to find more than a few items on a typical menu to meet their requirements. However, the home-cooked nature of the meals more than compensates for the laissez-faire attitude to calorie content and the dishes are wholesome, authentic and largely free from the constraints of processing or artificial additions. The city itself offers good food, good beer and good company.

Specialties and Local Producers

Like most major cities, the food in Prague covers the complete range of options from quick roadside bites to high-end gourmet

3 things you **must not** miss

◀ 1 Choco Story
This fascinating museum answers all your chocolate questions, as well as those you haven't even considered. *www.choco-story-praha.cz*

2 Prague Food Festival
This three-day May event is a celebration of the work of local chefs who demonstrate their skills. Food is in abundance so arrive with an empty stomach. *www.prague foodfestival.com*

3 Staropramen Brewery Tour
This Prague beer is now a common sight in bars all over the world. Take a look behind the scenes and find out how this famous brew makes its way into the bottle. *www.staropramen.com*

dining. The former takes on many guises but some of the most popular local snacks include the garlic-flavoured potato cake called *bramborák*, and grilled sausages (*klobasy*). Open sandwiches are another popular fast food and are typically served at delicatessens and cafes for lunch. Meat is the most popular dish for the main meal of the day, and Prague's restaurants usually serve this with dumplings, the favorite local side dish.

The Czech Republic is fanatical about its beer and Prague embraces the country's brewing heritage with aplomb. There is no shortage of beer halls, pubs and bars in which to sample the best of the local brew and Kozel's Medium is a particular favorite. There are also a number of microbreweries that combine the brewery, bar and restaurant in one venue. U Medvídků also has a museum for the complete beer education and sampling experience.

Markets and Shops

Prague is a gourmet haven and it's well worth scouring the city for the very best in meat, cheese, bread, beer and wine. The first stop should be Havelská Market where you can get your bearings, become attuned to the local specialties and embrace local life. Produce stalls play an important part in this outdoor shopping center but you will also find art, clothing and souvenirs. Then head off to one of the city's many quality delicatessens. Culineria Praha and Re Gourmet are two highly respected names.

Wine and beer are also in plentiful supply in Prague. The cellar at Monarch is legendary, and this prestigious shop in the old town also has a small bar where you can sample various drinks. Cellarius is also worth visiting for its good selection of Czech wines but, if your favor the grain over the grape, Galerie Piva is packed full of the best Czech and international beers.

WHERE TO EAT

LA DEGUSTATION
BOHÊME BOURGEOISE
Haštalská 18
Prague 110 00
t +420 222 311 234
w www.ladegustation.cz

This much-loved Prague dining destination offers guests sumptuous tasting menus that make the most of seasonal produce in a stylishly cavernous space.

ARTISAN
Rošických 603/4
Prague 5
t +420 257 218 277
w www.artisanrestaurant.cz

When a restaurant creates all of its own bread, pasta, stock and sauces from scratch you know that your meal is being prepared with care and attention. This tucked-away gem is the place to go for elegant food based on the freshest produce.

U RADNICE
U Radnice 2
Prague 1
t +420 224 228 136

This restaurant serves fantastic traditional dishes at reasonable prices. The rough-and-ready decor and communal dining tables allow diners the chance to indulge in some authentic Czech hospitality.

HAVELSKÉ TRZISTE

serves **4**

Garlic soup

Česnečka

CZECH CLASSIC

4 garlic cloves

1 tsp salt

5 cups (½ L) vegetable stock

1 tsp marjoram

1 tsp caraway seeds, crushed

2 medium potatoes, diced

2 Tbsp butter

Freshly ground black pepper

2 Tbsp freshly chopped parsley

Dark rye bread, to serve

Mash the garlic and salt together using a pestle and mortar or a fork.

Put the creamed mixture into a large saucepan and pour in the vegetable stock. Bring to the boil, then reduce the heat to a simmer. Add the marjoram, caraway seeds, potatoes and butter and simmer, uncovered, for about 20 minutes, until the potatoes are tender. Season with pepper and sprinkle chopped parsley on top.

Serve immediately with dark rye bread.

SLOVAKIA

SLOVAKIA SITS NESTLED between Poland to the north and Hungary to the south. The Carpathian Mountains spread across the north of the country, and the terrain is wild and beautiful although areas have been lovingly tamed to make way for ski resorts. Slovakia is very much an outdoors country and the food follows suit. Self-sufficiency was the norm in days gone by and the mountainous terrain necessitated the ability to produce and store one's own food supplies.

Milk remains a staple ingredient and its transformation into numerous other products ensures some variety in the diet. Meat is a vital source of protein and energy and pork, in particular, is included in many meals.
The meat is prepared in various ways, being used to make sausages, black pudding and smoked meat for the tough, cold winters. Dumplings, soups and potato dishes are other typical Slovak mainstays, and the ingenuity and creativity of the food makes it exciting.

travel essentials

TIME ZONE: GMT +1
TELEPHONE CODE: +421
CURRENCY: Euro
CAPITAL: Bratislava
LANGUAGE: Slovak

GETTING THERE: Bratislava is the international airport with flights operating to other European destinations. Many visitors arrive by train and there are plenty of services leaving from Prague and Vienna. Once inside the country, train is the preferred method of transport because there's a comprehensive rail network. If you drive, there is obviously greater flexibility with fast highways – just don't forget to buy the toll sticker.

Bratislava

Besides being the capital of Slovakia, Bratislava is the largest city in the country and its cultural, political and culinary focal point.

ABOVE Local- and foreign-grown hops are used in the many breweries in Bratislava.

OPPOSITE Stará Tržnica indoor market is the place the locals head to for their daily food shopping.

Bratislava lies on the extreme western side of the country, close to the borders of both Austria and Hungary. It straddles the banks of the River Danube, the many bridges allowing traffic and commerce to flow freely across. The city has been influenced by various adjacent countries and the influx of different peoples and cultures has modified the city's cuisine. Bratislava has always been open to the ingredients and dishes that have arrived from other parts of Europe, and this has helped shape the eating habits of the citizens. Although there are many staple foods and dishes, the city is an exciting blend of the best that Central Europe has to offer; the cuisine here is known as "Pressburg."

Specialties and Local Producers

Bratislava is a quirky culinary destination. While certain other European regions and cities cling on for dear life to their generations-old recipes and specialty dishes, this laid-back locale has happily acquired the best offerings from its neighbors, visitors and invaders to create a relative smorgasbord of dishes. This hybrid of Central European foods has been given a unique Slovakian twist, and these specialties and recipes have become part of the identity of the country.

There are, however, a number of foods that Bratislava claims for itself and they include a salad of cod, vegetables and mayonnaise called *treska*. Potatoes are a national staple and included in many meals. Tasty little cheese and potato dumplings (*bryndzové halušky*, see page 86) are made with sheep's cheese and are also a favorite in the city. Beer is popular and a number of breweries and brewpubs are located in the city, supplying the bars and restaurants with quality drinks. The Stein Brewery has been here for well over 100 years and is probably the most famous brand.

3 things you **must not** miss

◀ 1 Wine Tasting in Modra
Take a day trip from the city center and enjoy the fruits of Bratislava's vineyards. *www.tourist-channel.sk/modra*

2 Bratislava Food and Drink Festival
The best restaurants in the city get together to showcase their dishes with demos and tastings. *www.bratislava foodfest.sk*

3 Mamut Beer Hall
If you want to get a feel for the beer-drinking culture of the city, head to this enormous beer hall close to the old town. It is authentic, with beer aplenty and a big, brash, noisy atmosphere to accompany proceedings. *www.mamut.sk*

Markets and Shops

If you want to buy some of the beers sampled in the bars, Prešporská Pivotéka is a good place to start shopping. The shop is well stocked with the best Slovakian brew, as well as quality examples from other countries. Wine shops such as the incredible Vino Matyšák have the best selection.

There are also a number of indoor and outdoor food markets to choose from. Central Market Miletičova is a large affair that offers a wide range of fresh produce and other foodstuffs, as well as household goods. If there is a chill in the air, try Stará Tržnica in the old town. This is a compact indoor food market that is amply stocked with quality foods direct from the producers. Although the cuisine can, at first glance, appear to be heavily tilted towards the savory end of the palate, Bratislava has plenty to offer those with a sweet tooth. Čokoláda is a chocolate emporium that creates wonders with the bean, including an incredible selection of hot chocolates.

Cheese dumplings

Bryndzové halušky

SLOVAKIAN CLASSIC

serves **2–3**

2 large potatoes, peeled and finely grated

9 oz (250 g) all-purpose flour

9 oz (250 g) sheep's cheese

¼ lb (100 g) cooked bacon, finely diced

In a large mixing bowl, combine the potatoes and flour together.

Bring a large pan of salted water to the boil. Place the potato and flour mixture on a chopping board and form into tiny sausage shapes using your hands, or the back of a knife. They can be dropped straight into the boiling water.

Cook for a couple of minutes, or until the dumplings rise to the top of the pan. Use a slotted spoon to remove them to a large serving dish. Crumble the sheeps' cheese over the dumplings so it begins to melt, then sprinkle bacon on top and serve immediately.

POLAND

POLAND HAS AN impressive seven countries lining its borders (Russia, Lithuania, Belarus, Ukraine, Slovakia, Czech Republic and Germany) and yet it still manages to squeeze a substantial strip of coastline into its territory. The northern part of the country overlooks the Baltic Sea and ensures that the food is even more diverse than it might have been were Poland entirely landlocked. Its history has guaranteed an eclectic palate (Germany, Italy and Hungary are among the main influences) with spices and herbs being widely used, as well as dumplings and noodles. Soups make use of an incredible number of ingredients, rich meat stews are packed full of flavor and there's an endless array of sausages and cured meats filling delicatessens across the country. Pancakes, dumplings and bread soak up the sauces, and favorite desserts such as cheesecake (*sernik*) ensure that meals end on a sweet note.

travel essentials

TIME ZONE: GMT +1

TELEPHONE CODE: +48

CURRENCY: Zloty

CAPITAL: Warsaw

LANGUAGE: Polish

GETTING THERE: There are many rail routes from the likes of Amsterdam, Moscow, Prague and Vilnius. Warsaw is the major destination for air travelers although some European services, as well as internal flights, go to a number of other airports, including Krakow. Buses are a cheap means of internal travel, and for traveling into and out of the country. Ferries operate between Poland and the Scandinavian countries.

Kraków

Warsaw might be the capital city of this vast and diverse country but Kraków is the destination for food lovers.

This beautiful city in the south of the country draws its influences from a number of areas, but also has a staunchly held view of its own culture and identity. The wealth of cultural and architectural landmarks that scatter the area has made Kraków popular with tourists, and its rich history adds even greater kudos to the many churches, statues and great palaces.

The food of Kraków is both traditional and modern with a surprising amount of spices and other flavorings not often associated with central European cuisine. Typical dishes are still very much in vogue here, but a new generation of chefs and restaurants is making the city's cuisine more dynamic with cutting-edge restaurants celebrating Polish food in a new, exciting way.

Specialties and Local Producers

Some of the specialities of Kraków reflect the eating habits of the country as a whole, whereas others have originated here and subsequently gained popularity elsewhere. Potatoes and bread form the basis of the city's carbohydrate intake, and there are numerous specialty bakeries catering to a variety of tastes. Kraków claims to be the birthplace of the bagel and they have been baked to perfection in the city since the 17th century. They are eaten as a snack, being sold to hungry passers by from stalls on virtually every street corner.

3 things you must not miss

◀ 1 Wieliczka Salt Mines Tour
Takes visitors through a series of amazing carved chambers that are just a tiny part of the 185 mile (300km) long mine that produced table salt for hundreds of years. *www.salt minetours.com*

2 International Soup Festival
Chefs across the region compete for the title of best soup-maker in this unique and prestigious event. Combines food and music, and everyone can taste the results. *www.teatrkto.pl*

3 Bread Festival
This June event provides the opportunity for Kraków bakers to demonstrate their skills. Bread is a staple food and its creation is taken very seriously, although folk music and dancing ensure a party atmosphere. *www.krakow.pl*

Fermented cabbage sounds so much more appealing when it is referred to as sauerkraut, and this is another local favorite that is served as an accompaniment to main meals. Sausages are popular all over Poland but the smoked, seasoned pork sausage Krakowska takes its name from the city and is the Kraków version of the national favorite.

Wine production is still in its infancy in Poland, with beer the favorite drink. It has been brewed in the city for hundreds of years, resulting in a selection of very fine, highly rated lagers. Breweries such as C.K. Browar and Browar Jędrzejów are just a couple of the names to look out for. After beer, vodka is the tipple of choice and is generally drunk neat in small glasses, which is the best way to appreciate the subtle flavours of the different brands. Many Kraków bar owners have their own secret recipes for flavored vodkas, often using wild grasses and flowers.

Markets and Shops

Kraków offers a lively, authentic shopping experience and the Plac Nowy food market is a good place to start, with all manner of fresh food and other consumables on display. Stary Kleparz market is another great place to stock up on groceries direct from producers and to get a feel for the local culinary culture. A visit to the Jewish Quarter (Kazimierz) reveals a great deal about the checkered history of Kraków. This recently regenerated area is now a hub of retail and restaurant activity, and offers the food shopper a wealth of choice and diversity when buying groceries.

For anyone who appreciates the art of food, the stunning Krakowski Kredens will satisfy on every level. This emporium specializes in traditional Polish ingredients and recipes that have been tried and tested down the generations. For organic produce, Eco & Bio is well stocked while Szambelan offers a huge range of flavored vodkas.

WHERE TO EAT

POD ANIOŁAMI
Ulica Grodzka 35
31-021 Kraków
t +48 12 421 39 99
w www.podaniolami.com

The incredible 13th-century building houses a very impressive restaurant. No detail has been overlooked in either decoration or food presentation, and the traditional cuisine is worth every penny.

WIERZYNEK
Rynek Główny 15
31-008 Kraków
t +48 12 424 96 00
w www.wierzynek.com.pl

Despite its location in the main market square in the city, Wierzynek has no need to rely on passing trade. A traditional restaurant with an elegant interior, the restaurant serves some of the best Polish food in Kraków.

RESTAURACJA FARINA
Ulica Sw. Marka 16
31-017 Kraków
t +48 12 422 16 80
w www.farina.krakow.pl

This contemporary restaurant specializes in fish dishes but also serves the traditional flavors of Poland with a modern, Mediterranean flourish.

Easter cake

Babka

POLISH CLASSIC

serves **12–14**

Butter, for greasing
9 oz (250 g) all-purpose flour
1½ tsp baking powder
5 Tbsp cocoa powder
¾ tsp baking soda
1 tsp ground cinnamon
½ tsp salt
8 oz (225 g) butter
9 oz (250 g) superfine sugar

1 tsp vanilla extract
3 eggs
1 cup (225 ml) sour cream

FOR THE TOPPING:
5 oz (125 g) pecans, chopped
9 oz (250 g) plain chocolate chips
4 Tbsp superfine sugar
1 tsp ground cinnamon

Preheat the oven to 350°F/180°C/gas mark 4.

Butter a 10in (25cm) loaf cake pan. Sift together the flour, baking powder, cocoa powder, baking soda, cinnamon and salt in a large mixing bowl.

In a separate bowl, beat the butter and sugar together until it is light and fluffy. Add the vanilla extract and then beat in the eggs, one at a time.

Next add a little of the flour mixture to the creamed butter mixture. Then add a little of the sour cream. Repeat until the flour and sour cream have both been incorporated.

Combine the topping ingredients in a small bowl. Spread half the cake batter into the pan and sprinkle with half the crumb mixture. Pour in the remaining batter and sprinkle with the remaining crumbs. Using a knife, cut through the batter in a few places to ease the crumb mixture into the cake.

Bake in the oven for 35–40 minutes. Cover the top of the cake with aluminum foil and bake for a further 20 minutes until a skewer inserted into the center of the cake comes out clean. Allow the cake to cool, then carefully loosen it from the pan and turn onto a wire rack to cool.

LITHUANIA

LITHUANIA IS THE southernmost of the Baltic States, tucked under Estonia and Latvia, with a small length of coastline hugging the Baltic Sea. Scandinavia looms large to the north across the water, while Poland and Belarus are neighbors, bordering the south and the east of the country respectively. Nearly one-third of Lithuania is forested and the remainder features mountainous areas, lakes and wetlands and the mighty River Neman, so important for trade and transport. The climate is cool and is suited to agricultural produce with plenty of fresh vegetables and cereals being widely used.

Due to Lithuania's location, there's a degree of "crossover cuisine" with Scandinavia as well as the Eastern European countries that share its borders. The typical dumpling, pancake and meat dishes of the region are popular, as are dark rye bread, potatoes and pickles. Foraging is an important aspect of Lithuanian culture and although wild mushrooms and berries are rarely found in supermarkets, farmers' markets and roadside stalls are filled with this produce during autumn.

travel essentials

TIME ZONE: **GMT +2**

TELEPHONE CODE: **+370**

CURRENCY: **Litas**

CAPITAL: **Vilnius**

LANGUAGE: **Lithuanian**

GETTING THERE: Vilnius is the major international airport. There are a few smaller airports, mainly catering to budget airlines but most visitors tend to arrive in the capital. Trains run from Latvia, Poland and various cities in Russia. The relatively new road linking Vilnius to Tallinn is a fast, efficient way of traveling between the countries, and road travel within Lithuania itself is very straightforward.

Vilnius

Lithuania joined the EU in 2004 and has embraced its new identity as an important member state, with Vilnius – the European Capital of Culture in 2009 – at its center.

WHERE TO EAT

MEDININKAI

Aušros Vartu 8, Vilnius
t +370 600 86491
w www.medininkai.lt

A well-established eatery for sampling the local fare. The intimate dining area is sectioned into a number of separate rooms. The garden offers a charming alfresco space during the warmer months.

ŽEMAIČIAI

Vokieciu st. 24, Vilnius
t +370 5 261 6573
w www.zemaiciai.lt

Although a popular spot with locals and tourists, Žemaičiai makes a concerted effort to maintain its high standards and serves an extensive menu of Lithuanian and international dishes.

UŽUPIO PICERIJA

Paupio g. 3, Vilnius
t +370 5 5215 3666

This small, perfectly formed restaurant specializes in pizza cooked in wood-fired ovens and other simply cooked, tasty dishes.

The name of the capital of Lithuania derives from the Vilnia River, which flows through the country until it joins the Neris River in the city. Vilnius itself has a long, flowing history during which time it has been occupied by other countries and suffered great hardship and difficulties. Wandering through the city today, it is hard to appreciate the dark times because the capital has evolved into a major European center for culture and the arts.

The city's cuisine has also evolved over the years, and the hearty local food has been joined by an abundance of international flavors as ethnic restaurants have sprung up all over Vilnius and introduced people to new ideas. The locals' taste buds have been bombarded with heat and spice and local chefs have been inspired to veer off on an exciting tangent to create a new wave of modern Lithuanian cuisine.

Specialties and Local Producers

Bigos is a hearty meat and cabbage stew that is popular in Poland and other Eastern and Central European countries, but many sources claim that it originated in Lithuania. Whatever the case, there is no doubt that this is a Vilnius specialty and a dish that is served everywhere in the city. Dumplings are another popular item on the dinner menu, as is borscht soup, which is served cold in summer and hot in winter. As in many countries in the region, bread is a staple and in Vilnius that means rye bread, although bagels are also ubiquitous. Potatoes are cooked and prepared in every possible way (see page 94) while in autumn people visit stalls lining the roads on the outskirts of Vilnius to indulge the Lithuanian passion for wild mushrooms.

Vodka is the Vilnius answer to warming up on cold winter nights, and its purity

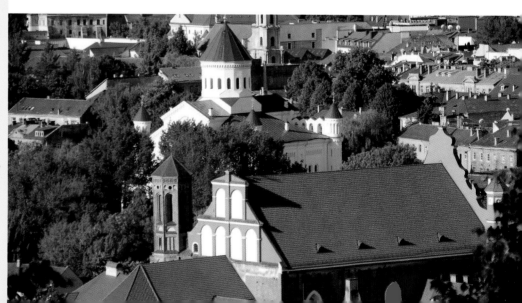

and quality is of the utmost importance. Trauktinė is a type of herbal vodka that is so highly rated that it was also used medicinally. If vodka doesn't tickle your taste buds, try *midus* (mead), an ancient local liqueur made from honey. Although it is generally served only at parties and special occasions, it is worth sampling while in Vilnius.

Markets and Shops

Vodka and mead might be readily available throughout the city but the Cognac Boutique ensures that Vilnius is also readily stocked with a wide range of high-end cognacs. With the luxury foodstuffs dealt with, it's time to head to the farmers' market with its vast array of fresh fruit, vegetables and local specialties. For a genuine Vilnius shopping experience, it would be hard to compete with Halès market in the old town. With a somewhat more haphazard layout than the precisely arranged produce of the Provençal or Tuscan markets, this is the way to experience the authentic Vilnius. This is where the locals come to do their food shopping and there are no airs or graces, just good honest bartering and bantering.

LEFT Wild mushrooms are sold at roadside stalls in August and September.

OPPOSITE ABOVE Borscht soup is served cold in summer and hot in winter in Vilnius.

OPPOSITE BELOW The old town in Vilnius is a charming enclave of medieval buildings and cobbled streets.

3 things you must not miss

1 Avilys Microbrewery
The only microbrewery in Vilnius, with three varieties to sample. Take a guided tour to find out exactly how the beer is brewed, before you sit down with a drink.
www.avilys.lt

2 Vilnius Walking Tour
Join a tour group or grab a map and take yourself around the city. Walking is the best way to see the highlights up close.

▶ **3 Kaziukas Fair**
This arts and crafts fair takes over the old town at the beginning of March. As well as handmade crafts, locally produced food, beer and spirits are on sale.

Dumplings stuffed with ground pork
Cepelinai
LITHUANIAN CLASSIC

serves **6**

FOR THE FILLING:

1 lb (450 g) ground pork

1 medium onion, peeled and finely chopped

1 tsp salt

¼ tsp pepper

1 large egg, beaten

FOR THE DUMPLING MIXTURE:

8 large baking potatoes, peeled and finely grated

2 large baking potatoes, peeled, boiled and mashed

1 medium onion, finely grated

1 tsp salt

Sour cream, to serve

Mix all the ingredients for the filling together in a large bowl. Set aside.

Place the grated potatoes in a piece of cheesecloth (or clean cotton dish towel) and squeeze over a bowl to get rid of the excess water. Pour off the water, reserving the potato starch at the bottom of the bowl.

Place the potatoes in a large mixing bowl with the reserved potato starch and add the mashed potatoes, onion and salt. Mix well.

Divide the potato mixture into six portions and mold each one into an even-shaped, circular patty. Place a large spoonful of the meat mixture in the center of a patty and then carefully pull up the sides of the potato mixture to make a ball shape. Seal all the edges. Repeat with remaining dumplings.

Bring a large pan of salted water to the boil. Carefully place the dumplings into the pan and cook for 25–30 minutes. Remove with a slotted spoon and drain on paper towels. Serve immediately with sour cream.

ESTONIA

ESTONIA IS A relatively small country, lying just south of Finland, which has played an important part in European history. It has been ruled by Germany, Denmark and Russia over the centuries but gained independence in 1920. However, it was occupied by the Soviet Union after the Second World War and it wasn't until 1991 that Estonia finally became an independent state. The country soon rediscovered its sense of identity and became part of the EU in 2004.

The identity of Estonia is partly shaped by food, and the countries that have played a part in its history still feature heavily in the cuisine. German and Russian dishes have become widely incorporated into everyday meals, while restaurants specializing in these cuisines are popular. However, Estonians have also developed their own dishes and specialties that have survived the various occupations and outside influences. Jellied meat, pickles, blood bread, curd, dumplings and a fruit and vegetable seasonal basket are just some of the highlights of this gutsy cuisine.

travel essentials

TIME ZONE: GMT +2

TELEPHONE CODE: +372

CURRENCY: Estonian Kroon

CAPITAL: Tallinn

LANGUAGE: Estonian

GETTING THERE: The two main airports in Estonia are Tallinn (on the mainland) and Kärdla (on the island of Hiiumaa). Both operate shuttle buses from the cities to the airport, which are just a few miles away. There are frequent ferry services to Finland, Germany and Sweden and an overnight train service to Moscow. The roads are good and it is possible to travel quickly and easily to nearby countries.

Tallinn

Since Estonia achieved independence Tallinn has seen a major increase in tourism, and rightly so.

ABOVE *Tallinn has a long brewing history and Saku is one of many famous local beers.*

OPPOSITE *The old town is a pleasant mix of shops, market stalls and cafes.*

Tallinn, in the north of the country, lies on the shores of the Gulf of Finland, just across the water from Helsinki. The stunning old town is still undergoing a series of regeneration works but it remains a beautiful and important addition to the architectural fabric of the city, the country and Europe. The walls, squares and original towers provide Tallinn with a real sense of historical importance: the past blends delightfully and seamlessly into the new modern city, a vibrant and exciting destination.

The food of Tallinn embraces the ingredients and produce of the country and has reignited a latent pride in the cuisine of the city, with local dishes and specialties taking center stage in Estonian eateries. However, recently there has been a definite shift with the modernization of the city, which has seen an influx of international restaurants.

Specialties and Local Producers

Estonians are big on curing, pickling and preserving and this will be immediately apparent to anyone visiting the city for the first time. Cuts of jellied meat, pickled cabbage and cured ham and sausages are never too far down a menu. Although some of the specialties, such as pigs' feet, might be a new experience to foreign diners, these are specialties for a very good reason and it's worth expanding your repertoire for a pleasant surprise. A particular favorite is a marinated eel dish, which is generally served cold. The proximity of Tallinn to the coastal regions of north Estonia means that fish is often on the menu and another local dish is *silgusoust*, a simple but delicious combination of Baltic sprats and bacon in sour cream.

Tallinn is proud of its brewing heritage and it produces an eclectic mix of drinks that are popular all over the Baltic states

3 things you must not miss

◀ 1 Õllesummer Beer Festival
The largest beer festival in the Baltics takes place in the old town. Although beer is the obvious draw, there is plenty of opportunity to learn more about Estonian culture including traditional music and other entertainment. www.ollesummer.ee

2 Kalev Chocolate Factory
This is essential visiting for anyone with even the faintest interest in chocolate and sweets. The museum is a step back in time with original display cabinets and heaps of information. www.kalev.ee

3 Jazzkaar Festival
The Tallinn International Jazz Festival is respected the world over for its comprehensive coverage. Get in the groove and loosen up with some local food and drinks while the performers take over the town. www.jazzkaar.ee

and further afield. Vana Tallinn is a sweet liqueur with a long list of ingredients including vanilla and cinnamon. The same brewery makes a range of flavored vodkas, while Saku beer is brewed just a few miles south of the city.

Markets and Shops

The Keskturg (Central Market) is where the locals buy their groceries and it offers fresh, local fruit and vegetables. Rotermann Square Farmers' Market has a good selection of organic food and NOP delicatessen is another great place to stock up on organic goodies. This trendy deli and cafe has salads, cakes and more.

Bonaparte is a gorgeous food complex with a well-stocked delicatessen, bistro, restaurant and award-winning cafe under one roof. Everything is homemade and there is an extensive selection of wines to try or buy.

If you want to make your own sandwiches, there are many top-quality bakeries in Tallinn. Fazer is a respected chain that has branches all over the city, as does Balti Sepik, another high-quality bakery with a good selection of breads and pastries. Pierre Chocolaterie has a number of cafes in Tallinn where you can sample wonderful handmade truffles and chocolates or sip a hot chocolate on chilly days.

WHERE TO EAT

VERTIGO
Rävala Puiestee 4
Tallinn
t +372 666 3456
w www.vertigo.ee

This aptly named restaurant sits at the top of a skyscraper with great views of the city below. The modern, sophisticated cuisine attracts the hip and trendy.

KULDSE NOTSU KÕRTS
Hotel St Petersbourg
Rataskaevu 7
10123 Tallinn
t +372 628 6500
w www.hotelst
  petersbourg.com/notsu-
  restaurant

The restaurant's aim is simple: to introduce customers to traditional Estonian cuisine in a light, airy, uncluttered dining room. It has achieved this with magnificent success and the food speaks for itself.

TROIKA
Raekojaplats 15
Tallinn
t +372 627 6245
w www.troika.ee

Dine in style in this classic eatery bathed in the glorious culinary history of Russia. The cavernous interior of this majestic restaurant is matched by the quality of the food.

Beet salad

Rosolje
ESTONIAN CLASSIC

serves **3–4**

1 salted herring

3 beets, boiled in skins

6 potatoes, boiled in skins

2 apples, peeled, cored and diced

4 dill pickles, finely chopped

2 hard-boiled eggs, diced

7 oz (200 g) cooked roast beef or pork, diced

FOR THE DRESSING:

¾ cup (175 ml) sour cream

1 tsp mustard

½ tsp sugar

¼ tsp pepper

2 Tbsp vinegar

Place the herring in a bowl of cold water, cover and leave in the refrigerator to soak overnight.

Clean and chop the herring. Peel the beets and potatoes, and dice. Place in a small bowl with the remaining salad ingredients and the chopped herring, and gently combine.

Mix all the dressing ingredients together in a small bowl and pour over the salad. Combine well and serve immediately.

HUNGARY

HUNGARY, ONE OF the oldest settled countries in Europe, has a history shaped by invasions (the Mongols), occupations (the Ottoman) and alliances. All, with the War of Independence, have had a major impact on the cultural and social evolution of the country. Geography has also played an important role, not least in the country's cuisine. Hungary has a diverse range of bordering countries, and it's no surprise that Slovakia, the Ukraine, Romania, Serbia, Croatia, Slovenia and Austria have all influenced the locals' taste buds. But Hungary's cuisine stands out in one important respect, the lavish use of paprika. The Hungarians have developed a taste for spices, and plenty of pungent and aromatic flavorings are used in all manner of dishes. Meat, soups and the traditional hearty stews, such as *pörkölt* and *paprikáscsirke*, are staple meals that represent the gutsy and flavorsome food of this culinary hotspot.

travel essentials

TIME ZONE: GMT +1

TELEPHONE CODE: +36

CURRENCY: Forint

CAPITAL: Budapest

LANGUAGE: Hungarian

GETTING THERE: Budapest is the main point of entry for Hungary, with Ferihegy Airport offering by far the most international travel options. Trains operate between Hungary and all its neighboring countries, but there are also services from Italy and Greece among others. A number of international bus routes also pass through, or terminate in, Hungary.

Southern Great Plain and Budapest

Hungary has a rich history, diverse culture and a distinctive cuisine that has resonated around Europe.

ABOVE The distinctive hot flavor in Hungarian food comes from paprika.

RIGHT Goulash is one of Hungary's most famous culinary exports.

OPPOSITE The flat plains are home to modern-day cowboys.

Although there are many cities and regions with a fine culinary heritage, the Southern Great Plain (or Puszta) is of particular note because it encapsulates a vast range of geographical areas and an interesting cultural mix. The fertile soil of the flat plains provides rich spoils, and the Hungarian cowboys live life much as they have done for hundreds of years. This is an ancient land that has only been lightly touched by tourism but it offers so much to anyone willing to get off the beaten track. You'll discover an authentic way of life and a cuisine to match; one that produces dishes that are rich, earthy and packed full of flavor with a level of heat that is unparalleled among indigenous European cuisines.

Specialties and Local Producers

There is one ingredient for which the Southern Great Plain is renowned all over the world, and that is paprika. The town of Kolocsa near the River Danube is the center

of paprika production in Hungary and, many would argue, the world. Here, the chilies are grown, harvested and transformed into the smoky spice that is redolent of Hungarian cuisine.

Gyula has a strong association with food. The famous Gyulai kolbász sausage comes from here and is regarded as one of the best Hungarian sausages. The town is also famous for its bakeries and

3 things you **must not** miss

◀ 1 Guided Tour of Zwack Fruit Brandy Distillery
The secret recipe might be well guarded but visitors can still have a nose around the distillery and find out how it is made. www.zwack.hu

2 Fishermen's Soup-cooking Festival in Baja
Each town has its own recipe, and the main square in Baja comes alive in July as thousands gather to eat soup and celebrate. www.hungary-tourist-guide.com/southern-great-plain.html

3 Gyula Baking Museum
Gyula is famous for its cakes and, although sampling them should be top priority, it is worth visiting the museum to investigate the local history of baking. www.cukraszok.hu/szazeves_to.htm

confectioners and boasts the second oldest confectioner in the country, Százéves Cukrászda. Pick salami is another great food from the Southern Great Plain and has been made in Szeged for nearly 150 years. Goulash (see page 102) and *pörkölt* are typical spicy meat stews of Hungarian origin and both were originally eaten by herdsman needing filling meals that were easy to prepare while out on the plains. Local paprika gave the dishes a dash of warmth and spice that transformed mere fodder into enjoyable food. The city of Kecskemét, with a reputation for stunning architecture and music, is also responsible for injecting a little warmth into the Hungarian diet thanks to its famous apricot brandy.

Markets and Shops

If Kecskemét is on your Hungarian itinerary, the daily farmers' market should provide ample raw ingredients for typical local dishes. Gyula also has a wonderful central market with stalls selling all manner of produce. The wine shop at Hotel Corvin in Gyula is a good place to check out local vintages.

Budapest is a food lover's paradise with the Great Market Hall providing an easy diversion from sightseeing with hundreds of stalls selling a disparate range of foodstuffs, from homemade pickles to fine wine. It's well worth taking the time to wander around. A number of organic markets, subject to very tight controls and regulations, supply produce direct from the farmers and include Albertfalvai Biomarket in XI district. Culinaris is a respected delicatessen stocking home-grown specialties, as well as choice products from around the world. Szamos is a confectioner with several branches around Budapest specializing in all things sweet.

WHERE TO EAT

● ● ● ● ● ● ● ● ● ● ● ● ● ●

✪✪✪
GUNDEL
Állatkerti út 2
Budapest 1146
t +36 1 468 4040
w www.gundel.hu

A Budapest institution that should be on the food map for anyone aiming to try a cross-section of restaurants in the city. Traditional Hungarian dishes are served in a fancy interior with all the pomp and ceremony that you would expect from the best in town.

✪✪
BOCK BISZTRÓ
Erzsébet Körút 43–49
Budapest 1073
t +36 1 321 0340
w www.bockbisztro.hu

For typical Hungarian dishes in a more laid-back environment, this ticks all the boxes. The elegant dining room is light and airy, and the food offers plenty of opportunity to sample the best of the region.

✪
CSALOGÁNY 26 ÉTTEREM
Csalogány u. 26
Budapest 1015
t +36 1 201 7892
w www.csalogany26.hu

Seasonal ingredients are the main feature at this unassuming local favorite where the quality is exceptional and prices extremely reasonable. Slightly off the beaten track, but well worth hunting down.

Goulash

Gulyás
HUNGARIAN CLASSIC

serves **2–3**

12 oz (350 g) chuck steak, diced

Flour, for dusting

2 Tbsp (25 g) butter

1 medium onion, roughly chopped

1 Tbsp paprika

1 medium red pepper, diced

1 x 14 oz (400 g) can chopped tomatoes

7 fl oz (200 ml) fresh beef stock

1 large potato, peeled and diced

¼ cup (50 ml) sour cream

Salt and freshly ground black pepper

Boiled potatoes or rice, to serve

Put the steak in a large bowl and sprinkle with the flour, mixing to coat evenly. Heat the butter in a large saucepan, add the steak and brown in the pan for a couple of minutes. Remove to a plate.

Add the onion to the pan and sauté for 5 minutes, until softened. Return the steak to the pan, sprinkle the paprika over and stir to coat the beef. Add the red pepper and stir again. Pour the tomatoes and stock into the pan, stir well to combine and bring to a simmer.

Cover the pan and simmer for 45 minutes, until the sauce has reduced and thickened and the beef is tender.

Add the potato to the pan and cook for a further 10–15 minutes, until cooked through. You might need to top up with a little water if the sauce has reduced. Stir in the sour cream, season and serve the goulash with boiled potatoes or rice.

CROATIA

A TURBULENT RECENT history has left Croatia scarred but it has dusted itself off and emerged as one of the most exciting and largely undiscovered European destinations. The Italians and Germans have long known of the natural beauty of the country's coastlines and historic towns, and it shouldn't be long before the rest of the world catches up, not least with Croatia's cuisine. The slim, lengthy coastline provides fantastic seafood, such as lobster, squid and octopus, all dressed with the lightest of Mediterranean touches. Meat, game and poultry are also popular, with goulash, pasta and dumplings regular items on the menu. And don't forget the famous truffles – culinary gold that dots the region of Istria.

travel essentials

TIME ZONE: GMT +1
TELEPHONE CODE: +385
CURRENCY: Kuna
CAPITAL: Zagreb
LANGUAGE: Croatian

GETTING THERE: The main international airport is outside the capital city, Zagreb, while the airports at Split, Pula and Dubrovnik are popular with tourists heading to the coastal areas. Driving is easy, road signs are good and new highways make car travel a breeze. Traffic between the cities is relatively light and the border crossings rarely involve lengthy delays. There are regular bus services to and from Italy.

Istria

Istria is a peninsula that juts into the Adriatic, with two of its borders consisting of coastline. The region shares its heritage with Italy and it is as close to the Italian mainland as to the rest of Croatia.

ABOVE *Istrian food markets are stocked with an abundance of fresh, local produce.*

RIGHT *Rovinj is a stunning town that is steeped in history and culture.*

OPPOSITE *Zigante Tartufi is the place to head to if you have a penchant for truffles.*

3 things you **must not** miss

◀ 1 Olive Oil Route

The region is famous for its olive oils and joining the Olive Oil Route is a great way to sample some of the best produce, while exploring some of the hidden areas of this beautiful part of the country. *www.istra.com/maslina*

2 Open Wine Cellars Day

On the last Sunday in May local winemakers open their doors to the public to help spread the word about the great wines currently being produced. *www.istria-gourmet.com/en/experiences/wine_tourism/wine_day*

3 Istria Truffle Festival

This October festival takes place in the village of Livade, where restaurateurs and truffle connoisseurs celebrate this wonderful ingredient. *www.istria-gourmet.com/en/experiences/istrian_truffle/truffles_days*

This influence is further exemplified by the fact that Istria became part of the Republic of Venice in the 13th century. The region was subsequently passed between Austria and Italy, and then became part of Yugoslavia after the Second World War. When Croatia gained independence in 1991, Istria was part of the new country. Given such a past, it would be easy to imagine a cuisine that was confused, eclectic or heavily influenced by Italy, and yet Istria has managed to keep its local foods as the main focus of its cooking.

Specialties and Local Producers

The vast and bountiful coastline of Istria has generated a wealth of seafood dishes. Many cafes and restaurants in coastal towns specialize in simple dishes, such as *škampi na buzara*, which combines fresh Adriatic prawns with tomatoes, garlic and parsley. Fish soup and grilled calamari also make frequent appearances on menus with plenty of olive oil and fresh vegetables to complement the Mediterranean-style diet.

Away from the coast, a rustic cuisine based on solid peasant food is still popular. Simple, seasonal ingredients are the order of the day but the flavors emanating from the apparently basic fare would put many top restaurants to shame. The Istrian larder is a treasure trove of quality ingredients, not least among them truffles. This is prime truffle-hunting territory and the pungent fungi are used in abundance on pasta and vegetable dishes. *Jota* is another Istrian specialty that makes use of the best local produce. This hearty soup is made from white beans, sauerkraut and potatoes. Istrian air-dried ham (*pršut*) is famous around the world and has protected status, and the olive oil of the region is also highly regarded. With such incredible ingredients, it is no surprise that this region is attracting food lovers from all over the continent.

Markets and Shops

Rovinj is one of the most beautiful towns in the country and it makes a great starting point for an Istrian exploration. The food market is full of the best local produce and is conveniently situated next door to the fish market. On the tip of the peninsula, the city of Pula is an important tourist destination, with its incredible Roman amphitheater and good shopping facilities. The farmers' market sells locally produced olive oil, wine and fresh produce, while truffle addicts should sniff out Zigante Tartufi for delectable examples of fresh pickings. Marino Wine Cellar has the best gourmet products of the region and, as the name suggests, there is an emphasis on wine.

WHERE TO EAT

✖✖✖
ZIGANTE
Livade-Levade 7
52427 Livade-Levade
t +385 52 664302
w www.zigantetartufi.com

This highly rated Istrian eatery embraces the ideas of the Slow Food Movement, ensuring that quality is always at the forefront. The menu is simple but exceptional, and the wine list extensive.

✖✖
GINA
Stoja 23
Pula 52100
t +385 52 387943
w www.gina-restaurant.com

This small restaurant with its charming, rustic interior serves up tasty homemade dishes influenced by different regions. They specialize in seafood and some tables have sea views too, making it a great place to indulge in quality, local food.

✖
FRA-KAT
Premantura 42
Pula 52100
t +385 52 575373
w www.fra-kat.co.cc

Fra-Kat is situated in a small village just outside Pula and it attracts a loyal local crowd of diners. They come for the wonderful fresh seafood that is cooked to perfection.

Fish stew

Brodeto

ISTRIA

serves 4

2 Tbsp olive oil

2 medium onions, chopped

3 tomatoes, peeled and chopped

2¼ lb (1 kg) mixed fish (such as pollock, haddock), cut into large strips

1 Tbsp white wine vinegar

Pinch of salt

1 tsp freshly ground black pepper

1 bay leaf

1 sprig of rosemary, leaves chopped

9 fl oz (275 ml) red wine

Polenta, to serve

Heat the oil in a large pan and sauté the onions over a medium heat for about 5 minutes.

Add the tomatoes to the pan, stir, then add the fish. Next, add the vinegar, salt, pepper, bay leaf and rosemary. Stir gently and slowly pour in the wine.

Bring to a simmer and cook gently, uncovered for 1 hour. Serve with polenta.

ROMANIA

ROMANIA IS A large, rural country with great swaths of forests and one of the largest river deltas on the continent, where the Danube flows into the Black Sea. The Carpathian Mountains jut up through the center of Romania and national parks encapsulate the beauty of the region. It is also an ancient country and, as if to prove the point, is where Europe's oldest human remains have been uncovered.

travel essentials

TIME ZONE: **GMT +2**

TELEPHONE CODE: **+40**

CURRENCY: **Leu**

CAPITAL: **Bucharest**

LANGUAGE: **Romanian**

GETTING THERE: There are a large number of airports in Romania, Bucharest being the largest, and more than 10 offer international flights. This makes it easy for travelers to fly directly to their preferred destination without having to make extra journeys. There are plenty of train services linking Romania to other countries and train travel is also the best bet when traveling inside Romania.

Bucharest

Although it is located in the south of Romania, Bucharest is at the center of the country in all other aspects. It is the capital, the largest city and the financial heart of the country.

ABOVE Most of the vast plum harvest is used to produce the spirit țuică.

RIGHT The grand Atheneum concert hall lies in the heart of the city center.

OPPOSITE Baklava is a popular sweet treat in Bucharest and all over the country.

3 things you **must not** miss

◀ 1 Caru' cu Bere Beer Hall
This impressive neoclassical building is the best place to sample a beer while checking out Bucharest's architecture. *www.carucubere.ro*

2 Bucharest Food Festival
Cookery demonstrations and producers selling traditional produce are just some of the delights at this October food fair. *www.bucharest foodfestival.ro*

3 Romanian Wine Tour
It would be a shame to travel to Bucharest and ignore the great local wines that are gaining an international reputation. There are a variety of tours from the city, lasting from a couple of hours to a number of days. *www.east adventures.com/tour-list/wine-tours-eastern-europe.html*

Bucharest has a great deal of architectural merit, which has always been quietly appreciated by the locals and tourists alike. More recently, however, its many attractions have started drawing an increasing number of visitors who are quickly spreading the word about this beautiful city.

The restaurants offer something for everyone, and the increased attention has had a positive effect on the quality and diversity of the eateries. It is possible to eat very well on a modest budget and Romanians are only too eager to share their culinary heritage with visitors. For those looking for fine dining, there is also a great deal of choice, with more and more high-end restaurants opening up in the city all the time, offering stiff competition for the best in neighboring European countries.

Specialties and Local Producers

The food of Bucharest is as varied and interesting as its history. There are influences from a number of different sources but the essential flavor of the Romanian diet lies at the heart of all the traditional cooking. Soups, stews, meatballs, sausages and stuffed vegetables (see page 110) are just some of the favorites, and in Bucharest it is possible to sample the best of them. The traditional barbecue is the ideal way to try the wonderful array of meat dishes, and Bucharest is known for its offal. *Caşcaval* and *telemea* cheeses are served with salads, while desserts are an important part of the meal. The rich, chocolate-layered tort Joffre was invented in a Bucharest restaurant and sticky, sweet *halva* and baklava are popular finishing touches.

Romania is one of the largest plum producers in the world, but the majority of the harvest goes toward the production of the favorite tipple, *ţuică*. If you do no more

than briefly step outside your hotel room during your stay in Bucharest, you will be familiar with this strong spirit, which is available in every bar, cafe and restaurant, and also in plenty of shops. It is often drunk as an aperitif or as an accompaniment to cheese and other snacks.

Markets and Shops

If you feel happier sticking to wine and leaving *ţuică* to the hardened drinkers, the well-informed staff at Vinexpert will guide you around the shop's extensive collection of Romanian wines. Gourmands looking for a tasty extra should browse the shelves of Delicateria Traiteur. The stunning displays include everything from meat and shellfish to chocolate and coffee.

For a more authentic taste of everyday shopping habits in Bucharest, head to the farmers' market in Piaţa Amzei. This is where locals come to barter with farmers and producers over the finest fresh fruit and vegetables. Piaţa Amzei is very central but if you want to experience the biggest outdoor food showcase in the capital, Piaţa Obor covers a huge area and sells produce, cheese, meat and much more. There are many other smaller food and flea markets around the city, including the weekend Târgul Ţăranului offering more specialized products and artisan goods.

WHERE TO EAT

✕✕✕
🍴 **BALTHAZAR**
Str. Dumbrava Rosie 2
Bucharest
t +40 21 212 14 60
w www.balthazar.ro

Balthazar attracts the who's who of Bucharest with its cool interior and exotic fusion cooking. A cocktail bar allows for a pre-dinner drink and the opportunity to turn a meal into an evening of culinary extravagance.

✕✕
🍴 **BABA DOCHIA**
Visarion 20
Bucharest

The service and food are universally saluted at this venue, which offers great value for money and consistently good plates of food.

✕
🍴 **LA MAMA**
Barbu Vacarescu 3
Bucharest
t +40 21 212 40 86
w www.lamama.ro

For authentic local food and wine in a buzzy, convivial restaurant, La Mama is hard to beat. Prices are very reasonable and the food is wholesome and tasty. With four restaurants dotted around the city, it's easy to find a good meal in a hurry.

Meat-stuffed zucchini

Dovlecei umpluti cu carne

ROMANIAN CLASSIC

serves **4**

4 zucchini

1 Tbsp olive oil

1 medium onion, finely chopped

2 garlic cloves, crushed

¾ lb (350 g) ground beef or lamb

Salt and freshly ground black pepper

1 x 7 oz (200 g) can chopped tomatoes

Sour cream or Greek yogurt, to serve

Preheat the oven to 400°F/200°C/gas mark 6.

Cut off both ends of the zucchini. Slice them in half and scoop out the seeds and pulp with a teaspoon. Place on a cookie sheet and bake for 15 minutes.

Heat the oil in a large frying pan and sauté the onion and garlic for 5 minutes. Add the meat to the pan, season well with salt and pepper and cook for 5 minutes, until browned. Add the chopped tomatoes and bring to a simmer for a couple of minutes, reducing the stuffing mixture to a thick consistency.

Spoon the stuffing into the zucchini and return to the oven for 15 minutes. Serve with sour cream or Greek yogurt.

BULGARIA

BULGARIA IS LOCATED on the Balkan Peninsula, with its eastern extreme on the Black Sea, the north bordered by Romania, the south by Turkey and Greece, and the west by Macedonia and Serbia. The cuisine of the country has many similarities with other Balkan countries, although it does have a rich agricultural tradition resulting in a greater use of fresh vegetables. Rearing animals is widespread leading to plenty of meat on the menu and a wide variety of milk products. Today, the traditional salads and meat dishes of the past have been reinvented in the restaurants of Sofia and other towns and cities. The numerous staple dishes provide a fantastic basis for the creation of a contemporary take on Bulgarian cuisine.

travel essentials

TIME ZONE: GMT +2

TELEPHONE CODE: +359

CURRENCY: Lev

CAPITAL: Sofia

LANGUAGE: Bulgarian

GETTING THERE: Train travel is a popular way to explore Bulgaria from neighboring countries, and there are overnight services from the likes of Vienna and Bucharest. There are also four international airports; some have been monopolized by budget airlines and new routes are cropping up all the time.

Sofia

Sofia's coffee culture appeals to visitors looking for a combination of sightseeing and people-watching, and a city break here can be as vibrant or as low-key as you want.

ABOVE Sirene *is a cheese similar to feta that is used in many Bulgarian recipes.*

RIGHT Banitsa *pastries are typical of the region and are often stuffed with cheese.*

OPPOSITE Alexander Nevsky *Cathedral is one of the most famous landmarks in Sofia.*

Sofia is an ancient city and the boundary walls, dating back to the 7th century, prove it. The city lies in a huge valley, at the foot of Mount Vitosha and is located in the western part of Bulgaria. Sofia has a pleasing mix of architectural styles that have been added in layers over the centuries to create this romantic but functional capital.

In keeping with many other European countries, bread and potatoes are the starting block for many meals, and numerous dishes are pepped up with paprika. The markets spill over with luscious fresh fruit and vegetables, and dairy produce is in abundance.

Specialties and Local Producers

Mealtimes are big social events and often involve a number of courses consumed over a lengthy period of time, accompanied by a fairly generous serving of alcohol. Which is where we begin. Wine, beer and spirits are all popular in Sofia and wine-making is an ancient tradition, with regions including the Struma River Valley to the south of Sofia producing high-quality vintages. *Mastika* is a local brew that certainly isn't for the faint-hearted. Similar to ouzo, this potent spirit is usually served as a celebratory toast. *Rakia* is another local

3 things you **must not** miss

◀ 1 Cafe at the Archaeological Museum

The perfect way to soak up culture and cuisine in the same outing. The museum houses an incredible collection of artifacts while the Art Club Museum Cafe is the coolest place to hang out in town. *www.naim.bg*

2 Bulgarian Wine Tasting

In order to appreciate the range and complexity of the wines on offer here, a wine tasting is essential. Many shops and wineries offer free sips, including Todoroff Wine Cellar. *www.todoroff-wines.com*

3 Park Live Festival

This annual music festival offers the chance to see local musicians strut their stuff and sample some of Sofia's great street food. *www.parklive fest.com*

firewater, made with fermented fruit, and variations can be found all over this part of Europe.

Cheese is used with liberal abandon in Bulgarian cooking, and salads are often adorned with a block of *sirene*, either whole or crumbled. *Shopska* salad (see page 114) is a popular local specialty that includes *sirene*, as well as peppers, onions and tomatoes and it can be eaten as a starter or a light lunch. *Banitsa* pastries are often stuffed with cheese while stuffed peppers are a popular cafe dish in Sofia. The rich pork stew called *kavarma* is another must-try with its paprika kick and rich, thick sauce.

Markets and Shops

The markets of Sofia are a bustling, buzzing affair and there are plenty of them. People shop daily to ensure that they are using fresh, quality produce. Graf Ignatiev farmers' market sees producers from around the region competing to sell their fresh fruit and vegetables. Locals arrive early to get the best choice and there is always a good selection on offer. Women's Market (Zhenski Pazar) is another great place to soak up the local atmosphere. This vast site is largely dedicated to food but there are plenty of random utility and souvenir stalls offering items that you never knew you needed. If the noise and congestion of the food markets gets a little too much, try the Central Hali Shopping Center where the ground floor is given over to produce and the upstairs to a range of quick-fix eateries. When you've finished shopping, head to Todoroff or the Kehlibar Wine Cellar for a good selection of Bulgarian wines and spirits.

WHERE TO EAT

● ● ● ● ● ● ● ● ● ● ● ● ●

POD LIPITE
1 Elin Pelin Str
Sofia
t +359 2 886 50 53
w www.podlipitebg.com

This delightful rustic hideaway draws hungry, appreciative patrons in droves to taste the best Bulgarian cuisine in the city.

✖✖
NINO
47 Cherkovna Str
Sofia
t +359 88 400 0606
w www.nino-bg.com

A carefully designed restaurant, from the furnishings to the menu. The food is based around classic Bulgarian cuisine with fresh ingredients at the fore.

MANASTIRSKA MAGERNITSA
67 Han Asparuh Street
Sofia
t +359 2 980 3883
w www.magernitsa.com

This elegant eatery serves traditional Bulgarian food at affordable prices. The recipes have been collated from monasteries around the country for a truly authentic and quirky take on the classics.

White cheese and tomato salad

Shopska

SOFIA

serves **4**

4 scallions, trimmed and thinly sliced

4 large tomatoes, cut into eight

1 cucumber, trimmed and sliced

1 green pepper, seeded and cut into rings

1 red pepper, seeded and cut into rings

2 Tbsp vinegar

4 Tbsp olive oil

Salt and freshly ground black pepper

½ lb (225 g) Bulgarian white cheese or feta

Freshly chopped parsley, to serve

Place all the ingredients, apart from the cheese and parsley, in a large mixing bowl and combine well, ensuring that the vinegar and oil cover all the vegetables.

Transfer the salad to individual serving plates and sprinkle some crumbled or grated cheese over each plate. Sprinkle with chopped parsley to finish.

GREECE

THE FOOD OF Greece is intrinsically linked to its culture and history. This ancient civilization has held its cuisine close to its heart for thousands of years and we have the surviving texts of some of the great philosophers and poets to prove it. Homer makes many references to food and wine in his great works *The Iliad* and *The Odyssey*, and the importance of food to the Greek culture is as relevant as it was millennia ago.

Greece is a magical place filled with myths and legends, and the landscape is equally stunning. Whitewashed buildings dot the harbors and hillsides, simple tavernas serve memorable meals and ancient monuments bring history back to life.

travel essentials

TIME ZONE: GMT +2
TELEPHONE CODE: +30
CURRENCY: Euro
CAPITAL: Athens
LANGUAGE: Greek

GETTING THERE: Athens airport is a huge international affair and the hub of the country's travel system. Most people arrive here, although other options include boats from various points in Turkey, Italy and the Greek islands. Ferries operate to many islands but timetables can change, so it's important to check details before you travel.

Peloponnese

The Peloponnese lies at the southernmost part of mainland Greece and its indented coastline gives it the appearance of a giant hand stretching its fingers into the warm Mediterranean sea.

WHERE TO EAT

✖✖✖
TAKIS FISH TAVERNA
Lemini
Peloponnese
t +30 27 3305 1327

The food is so well executed that the place is packed every night and its reputation is spreading fast.

✖✖
TAVERNA PRAXITELOUS
7 Spiliopoulou
Olympia
t +30 26 2402 3570

Attached to the hotel of the same name, this restaurant serves top-quality Greek fare in a dining room that is packed with appreciative locals.

✖
DIETHNES
Paleologou 105
Sparta 23100
t +30 27 3102 8636

The home-cooked dishes in Diethnes have made this harbor-front venue a popular restaurant. Prices are reasonable and the food is lovingly prepared from the best ingredients, with seafood the specialty.

Clusters of beautiful islands are scattered in the vast expanse of water surrounding this wonderful region that basks in the sun. It would be an island were it not for the connection in Corinth to the mainland.

The sea provides the area with much of its food and bustling fishing villages and harbors line the coast, where small boats supply local restaurants with their daily specials. Away from the sea, olive groves, vines and fruit trees are permanent fixtures on the landscape. The region's many food products have helped earn it the title "The Garden of Greece."

Specialties and Local Producers

The southern town of Kalamata is famous for its olives, which are so good that they have been awarded Protected Designation of Origin status. The honey from the region is among the finest in the country and everyone knows that Greek honey is among the best in the world. In Mani – the middle section of the peninsula – food is a force to be reckoned with. The preserved meats are renowned for their taste and quality, and the pork is salted and smoked over cypress wood to provide its unique flavour. Mani sausages are also a talking point, and

3 things you **must not** miss

1 Agritourism Fair in Epidavros

This annual July food fair is organized by local farmers and producers to bring their products to the people. *www.epidavros.cc*

2 Mercouri Estate

This stunning winery near Pyrgos provides a memorable excursion. There is plenty to see in the visitor center and winery, while the location is also incredible and well worth the journey. *www.mercouri.gr*

▶ 3 Artichoke Festival in Iria

It may seem alien to some people to celebrate a vegetable, but it's a fine specimen and a great excuse to have a party. This annual event sees folk music and dancing as well as plenty of dishes featuring the star of the show.

various ingredients are used to distinguish the region's pork sausages from other varieties. Even the monks in the Peloponnese get their hands dirty in the kitchen. Those living in the Taxiarchon Monastery in Lakonia spend a month of the year preparing rose-petal jam from flowers grown around the grounds. It is a local delicacy and the limited number of jars are soon snapped up by savvy locals. The Peloponnese is also a wine-producing region with the areas of Mantinia and Nemea both known for their quality products. The ancient wine retsina is also produced in various locales in the region.

Markets and Shops

There are too many markets to mention in the Peloponnese. Needless to say, if you are self-catering you'll have no problem making an authentic Greek meal. Kalamata has a daily produce market, as well as a farmers' market supplying fresh vegetables, citrus fruits, meats, cheese and, of course, olives. Most towns and villages have their own markets supplying the best from the local area, and there are plenty of specialist shops and food stalls if you need extra supplies. Kotsiopoulos Bros Butchery in Ano Agora, Tripoli, is famous for its roast

suckling pig, the Olive Oil Museum in Sparta sells a range of olive oil products (as well as offering a fascinating insight into the production of this local specialty) and the Mercouri Estate in the west of the region also produces some delicious olive oil, as well as plenty of decent wines, which are available to try and buy.

OPPOSITE ABOVE The town of Kalamata is famous the world over for its olives.

OPPOSITE BELOW The harbor town of Gythio exudes Greek charm and natural beauty.

BELOW The monks in Lakonia produce rose-petal jam just one month of the year.

Athens

Athens is a frenetic, overcrowded and fast-paced city that is steeped in history but very much involved in the workings of modern Europe.

ABOVE Feta is a staple ingredient in Greek cuisine, particularly when it comes to salads and other cold dishes.

OPPOSITE The Parthenon ensures the history of Athens is never far from the minds of visitors.

The largest city in Greece sits in the south of the country, to the east of the Peloponnese, and it acts as a gateway to the beautiful, numerous islands of the Aegean. However, the capital city couldn't be more different from the laid-back, traditional lifestyle that exists on these islands. The juxtaposition between the ancient and modern is obvious throughout the city, as famous monuments, such as the Parthenon, share the same area as the incredible Olympic Stadium. Modern architecture is treated with as much respect as the old, and the same attitude applies to the city's food. While traditional recipes and foods remain an important part of everyday life in Athens, locals are also keen to embrace the many new and exciting restaurants that are now springing up.

Specialties and Local Producers

Athens is one of the oldest cities in the world and as such it has seen a constant stream of people arriving and leaving over the course of its lengthy history. Whether from the islands, the countryside or abroad, all have left their mark on the city and many culinary specialties from other regions around the country have been adopted. There are, however, a number of staple foods that are enjoyed in the capital with particular gusto, and feta cheese is right at the top of the list. This distinctive, salty cheese is served with a number of dishes, most notably Greek salad.

Meat is popular and the local *mprizoles* are one of the favorite ways to eat beef or lamb, simply cooked with lemon juice and olive oil. The olive is another staple ingredient and whether it is eaten as is, or with the oil extracted, it will appear on most dishes in some form. Attica (the Athens region) produces great quantities of quality oil, which is eagerly devoured by taverna

3 things you must not miss

1 Food Market Walking Tour

See the best parts of the city with an experienced guide. If you have a limited schedule or just want to get the low-down on the market and city center, a walking tour is the ideal solution. *www.athens tours.net*

2 Dionysia Greek Wine Festival

This festival is the perfect opportunity to hone your Greek wine knowledge and there is plenty to learn about. Producers from across the country come to show off their products. *www.greece-athens.com*

3 Athens and Epidaurus Festival

This huge cultural festival is the highlight of the Athens calendar and lasts from May to August, when events are held in different parts of the city on a daily basis. *www.greekfestival.gr*

✖✖✖
VAROULKO
80 Piraios
Athens
t +30 210 522 8400
w www.varoulko.gr

This fish restaurant has come a long way and impressed a great number of people on its journey to becoming one of the greats of the Athens dining scene.

✖✖
BALTHAZAR
27 Tsocha Street
Ambelokipi
Athens
t +30 210 641 2300
w www.balthazar.gr

This ultramodern eating and drinking venue has struck just the right chord with the locals. The food is unpretentious but well executed and the vast interior has been cleverly designed.

✖
DAMIGOS
41 Kidathinaion
Plaka
Athens
t +30 210 322 5084
w www.mpakaliarakia.gr

A local institution that has been cooking up its delicious codfish specialty for appreciative diners for well over 100 years. The wine is brought directly across from the family-owned vineyard and the whole experience is personable and authentic.

and restaurant diners. The retsina of the Attica region is also prominent in the bars of Athens, although this distinctive Greek wine is now competing against the high-quality vintages being produced by vineyards around the country.

Markets and Shops

Athens markets are a wonderful agglomeration of color, noise and potential confusion for the visitor. The Central Market is a huge collection of stalls and food huts selling everything a kitchen could require. As well as the usual fresh fruit and vegetables there is a fish market and a number of established butchers. There are also huge displays of locally grown olives and a shop in the middle of the market is dedicated to the fruit. At the Olive Shop of Sabbas Psychogios you can sample before buying.

In Athens, farmers' markets (*laiki*) aren't specialist weekly events: they take place all over the city, all the time. They are the most convenient way for producers to sell their food to the public, and a weekly event won't suffice when shopping is done on a daily basis.

Meat and macaroni pie

Pastitsio

GREEK CLASSIC

serves **4**

1 Tbsp olive oil

1 onion, chopped

2 garlic cloves, finely chopped

1 lb (450 g) ground lamb

2 celery stalks, chopped

2 Tbsp tomato purée

1 x 14 oz (400 g) can chopped tomatoes

½ tsp ground cinnamon

1 tsp chopped fresh thyme

1 tsp chopped fresh oregano

1 bay leaf

¾ cup (175 ml) white wine

¾ lb (350 g) macaroni

FOR THE WHITE SAUCE:

1 Tbsp (15 g) butter

1 Tbsp (15 g) all-purpose flour

1¼ cup (300 ml) whole milk

½ cup (50 g) Kefalotiri or Parmesan cheese, grated

Heat the oil in a large frying pan, add the onion and garlic and fry over a medium heat for 2–3 minutes. Add the lamb and celery and increase the heat. Fry for about 5 minutes.

Add the tomato purée, chopped tomatoes, cinnamon, herbs and wine to the pan, bring to the boil and simmer for 20 minutes. While this is simmering, cook the macaroni in a large pan of boiling, salted water, according to the package instructions. Drain well.

Preheat the oven to 350°F/180°C/gas mark 4. Make the white sauce. Using a fork, mix together the butter and flour. Place in a small pan over a low heat and, when the butter has begun to melt, gradually pour in the milk. Stir constantly until all the milk is used and the sauce has thickened.

Place alternate layers of macaroni and the meat mixture into a 2 qt (2 L) ovenproof dish. Pour the white sauce over the pasta and finish with the grated cheese. Bake in the oven for 30 minutes.

White bean soup

Fasolada

GREEK CLASSIC

serves **4–6**

1 lb (450 g) white beans

3 Tbsp olive oil

1 onion, finely chopped

3 carrots, finely chopped

3 tomatoes, peeled, seeded and diced

1 medium potato, peeled and diced

2 celery stalks, sliced

Salt and freshly ground black pepper

Soak the beans in water overnight.

Drain and rinse the beans. Bring a large pan of water to the boil and boil the beans for 10 minutes. Drain well.

Heat the olive oil in a large pan and add the beans. Add the onion, carrots, tomatoes, potato and celery to the pan and season with salt and pepper. Stir the mixture and add enough water to cover the beans by about 1 in (2½ cm).

Bring to the boil then cover and simmer the soup for about 1½ hours. If the beans are still hard, cook for a further 20–30 minutes. The beans should be tender but still intact. Season to taste with salt and pepper.

TURKEY

TURKEY IS AT the geographical divide between Europe and Asia, and lies at the southeastern extreme of the European continent. This coexistence of diverse cultures has resulted in an extraordinary country that encapsulates elements of both 'East' and 'West'. The colorful bazaars of Istanbul are like nothing else in Europe and the many spices sold are widely used in Turkish cuisine, which has its roots in the Middle East and Central Asia, although there are also classic Mediterranean touches. Yogurt is used in many dishes, including *cacık* (a mint and yogurt dip), while pastries, such as *börek*, are standard Turkish fare. The food is regional with a cosmopolitan slant in Istanbul and the cuisine is quite unlike anything else in Europe.

travel essentials

TIME ZONE: **GMT +2**

TELEPHONE CODE: **+90**

CURRENCY: **New Turkish Lira**

CAPITAL: **Ankara**

LANGUAGE: **Turkish**

GETTING THERE: Istanbul and Ankara airports operate international services but Istanbul is the most likely entry point. Some people choose to drive from other European countries using the border crossings from Bulgaria and Greece. The boat is still a popular route into the country, with Bodrum being the main port.

Istanbul

Istanbul is one of the most densely populated cities in Europe. It is also one of the most exciting and vibrant to visit, with its wealth of centuries-old architecture and its vast cultural heritage.

ABOVE Traditional Turkish delight is a sweet treat made with nuts and fruits.

RIGHT The street stalls in Istanbul sell all manner of snacks and delicacies.

OPPOSITE Mısır Çarşısı spice market is an array of intoxicating color.

It represents the border between the continents of Europe and Asia and shares its geographical location and culture with both. Having previously been at the center of the Roman and the Ottoman Empires, it has acquired the highlights of many cultures and enjoyed a privileged status.

Istanbul is a heady mix of extremes: the weather turns from high summer temperatures to winter snow; the culture is

3 things you **must not** miss

◀1 Karaköy Güllüoğlu Baklava Factory Tour
This famous sticky dessert is renowned the world over, and the Karaköy Güllüoğlu tour explains the ancient and skilled art of creating these sumptuous sweets.
www.gulluoglu.biz

2 Walking Tour of Istanbul Bazaars
The bazaars provide some of the most memorable experiences in Istanbul and you will discover more about the history of these incredible markets on an escorted tour.
www.turkeytravelplanner.com

3 Learn the Secrets of Turkish Cooking
There are a number of cookery courses in the city, suitable for everyone from novice to expert. A great way to follow up a trip to the bazaars. www.cooking alaturka.com

a mix of the old and the new; and the food is either passionately authentic or decadently contemporary. Istanbul is uniquely placed to offer visitors a glimpse of merging cultures and emerging food trends in one location.

Specialties and Local Producers

The coffee shops and tea houses of Istanbul are legendary, and this passion for hot drinks has persisted for centuries. The ritual of drinking coffee is matched by the ritual of preparing it, and cafes such as Fazıl Bey'in still prepare the drink in the traditional way. Coffee is often served with another specialty, Turkish delight (*lokum*). The best examples of this ubiquitous Turkish sweet are made entirely from fruit and nuts and bear little resemblance to the fake, sugary jellies most visitors from abroad are used to.

The location of Istanbul, straddling the Bosporus Strait, means that seafood is another local specialty and a simple fish sandwich (*balık ekmek*) is one of the best ways to enjoy some fresh, locally caught fish. The sandwiches are available from street vendors or from harborside cafes, where you can enjoy a more sophisticated version. *Katıklı* is another local favorite: this flatbread is layered with yogurt, spinach, spices and other fillings and is perfect for a quick lunch. Roasted chestnuts and corn from street stalls make delicious snack foods, thick *kanlıca* yogurt is an Istanbul obsession and authentic kebabs served with yogurt dip (*cacık*, see page 124) should be sampled at every opportunity.

Markets and Shops

Going shopping in Istanbul is like no other grocery trip in the world. The bazaars of the city center are a gorgeous assault of noise

and color emanating from the narrow, winding streets. Visitors are carried along helplessly with the more focused regulars, entranced and distracted by the myriad stalls and their incredible displays. The Kapalıçarşı is one of the largest covered markets in the world with separate areas for different products. This is the place to come for spices and exotic foodstuffs but it's difficult not to be distracted by the ornate jewelry, carpets and clothing. Mısır Çarşısı is slightly smaller in size but no less impressive, and this spice market is a food lover's emporium with its piles of colorful spices.

For a less frenetic shopping experience, Erzincanlılar is one of the best delicatessens in Istanbul and Antre Gourmet stocks a good selection of local cheeses, as well as bread, olive oil and other treats. Savoy Pastanesi sells ornate celebration cakes, mouthwatering biscuits and macaroons while the Çinaralti teahouse is the place to quench your thirst after a successful shopping spree.

WHERE TO EAT

✦✦✦
MIMOLETT
Sıraselviler Caddesi, 55
Istanbul
t +90 212 245 9858
w www.mimolett.com.tr

This is high-end dining at the hands of experienced chef Murat Bozok. The modern Mediterranean cuisine is delightfully presented in a historic building.

✦✦
SUNSET GRILL & BAR
Adnan Saygun Caddesi,
Yol Sokak 2, Ulus Parkı
Istanbul
t +90 212 287 0357
w www.sunsetgrillbar.com

It is difficult not to be seduced by the location and stunning views from this city-center eatery. The fusion menu of Japanese and Turkish fare lives up to the high standards set by the design team.

✦
HACI ABDULLAH LOKANTASI
Ağa Camii
Atıf Yılmaz Cad.
No: 9/A 80070
Beyoğlu / Istanbul
t +90 212 293 8561
w www.haciabdullah.com.tr

This is the place for a real taste of authentic Turkish cuisine. The restaurant is located in the fascinating Beyoğlu district, which is steeped in history.

Yogurt and cucumber dip

Cacık

TURKISH CLASSIC

serves **8–10**

2 cucumbers, peeled and grated

2 garlic cloves, minced

Salt

1 pt (600 ml) natural yogurt

1 Tbsp freshly chopped mint

Extra-virgin olive oil, to serve

Fresh crusty bread, to serve

Combine the cucumber and garlic in a large mixing bowl. Season with salt to taste.

Add the yogurt to the bowl and mix well. Transfer to a serving bowl. Sprinkle with the mint and drizzle a little olive oil on top. Serve immediately with bread.

UNITED KINGDOM

OVER RECENT YEARS there has been a surge of interest and pride in indigenous British produce and cuisine. In restaurants around the country, history and modernity have merged on the dining table. Classic dishes and ingredients have been given a fresh lease on life and a contemporary twist and, as a result, British cuisine has developed a new, exciting identity.

From rare-breed livestock farms to artisan cheese makers, the UK is teeming with dedicated and passionate food producers who believe in their products and are successfully spreading this enthusiasm to their customers. There has been a quiet but unprecedented food revolution as producers reignite generations-old processes, recipes and skills to create food that is unique to Britain.

For their part, consumers are taking an ever-greater interest in the story behind their shopping basket. Farmers' markets are thriving, as are independent food shops, delicatessens, quality butchers and cheesemongers. After hiding under a bushel for far too long, British food is now being championed, appreciated, enjoyed and recognized both at home and abroad.

travel essentials

TIME ZONE: GMT

TELEPHONE CODE: +44

CURRENCY: Pound Sterling

CAPITAL: London

LANGUAGE: English

GETTING THERE: With five international airports serving London and over 20 more regional airports around the UK, it is possible to fly fairly close to your desired destination. Eurotunnel provides further options for traveling from mainland Europe, while ferry ports around the coast offer frequent services to and from Ireland, France and Spain.

Angus and Dundee

Angus is a region in the central, eastern part of Scotland on the North Sea coast. The area borders Dundee, the fourth-largest city in Scotland.

Angus is an area that encompasses the traditional ideas of a rugged Scotland, full of undiscovered wilderness and vast, open spaces. It's also home to vibrant, modern urban centers. The history and traditions of Angus are kept to the fore, while it continues to shine as an important tourist destination with millions of visitors

3 things you **must not** miss

◄ 1 Arbroath Sea Fest
This annual festival celebrating the sea takes place in August and offers the chance to overdose on Arbroath smokies and other local delicacies. Cookery demonstrations, music and street theater fill the gaps between meals.
www.arbroathseafest.co.uk

2 Get Close to Nature on an Angling Trip
Angus and Dundee are renowned for their fantastic angling opportunities and this is a great way to see some stunning countryside while hooking a few fish.
www.anglingtayside.com

3 Dundee Flower and Food Festival
This annual September event is a celebration of color with hundreds of flower species on display and guest chefs on hand to provide the food.
www.dundeeflowerandfood festival.com

flocking to the natural beauty of the lochs and mountains.

Scottish cuisine has enjoyed a recent flourish of interest. Farmers and producers have welcomed the chance to show off their produce and the great British public has realized that a whole host of incredible products are available, quite literally, on its doorstep.

Specialties and Local Producers

Scotland is known the world over for the quality of its beef and lamb, both of which have been given Protected Designation of Origin status. Scottish farmed salmon has been accorded the same honor and this highly regarded, sustainable fish can be bought worldwide. The coastal town of Arbroath is famous for haddock. The fish are salted, dried overnight and then smoked in special barrels to create Arbroath smokies. Top chefs are now singing the praises of the smokie and these delicious subtly flavored fish are now widely available. Angus is heavily involved in the Slow Food Movement and this has undoubtedly helped ensure the integrity of the food produced in the region. Farmers and producers are committed to the integrity of traditional farming methods and

animal rearing to produce food that is unique to the region. Whisky is also produced all over the country and a number of companies are located around the Angus area. The Glencadam Distillery in Brechin produces a number of single-malt whiskies of varying ages.

Markets and Shops

The food of Angus is a source of great pride, and the farmers' markets in the area allow locals and visitors to buy directly from the producers. Both Angus and Dundee have flourishing farmers' markets where all manner of local produce, meat and seafood can be bought.

Farm shops are another way of purchasing local produce on a regular basis and the region has a fine selection of shops, many of which are located on the farm premises. Milton Haugh Farm Shop specializes in fresh seasonal produce, as well as a good selection of meat and game and The Cheesery in Dundee is an award-winning independent cheese shop, which also stocks other deli products. Sugar and Spice in Arbroath is an old-fashioned confectionery store with a fudge factory on the premises, and also a delightful tearoom and restaurant.

WHERE TO EAT

GORDON'S RESTAURANT
Main Street
Inverkeilor DD11 5RN
t +44 1241 830364
w www.gordons
    restaurant.co.uk

This much-lauded restaurant's menu is based on seasonal Scottish ingredients. The father-and-son team have earned themselves a number of awards for their cooking.

THE BLUE MARLIN
9 Reform Street
Monifieth DD5 4BA
t +44 1382 534001
w www.thebluemarlin.co.uk

People travel here from far and wide to sample the best in Scottish seafood. A bland entrance hides a tucked-away culinary gem.

MERCURY MAIA
Dundee Carlton Hotel
2 Dalgleish Road
Dundee DD4 7JR
t +44 1382 462056
w www.dundeecarlton.com

The unusual name comes from a record-breaking seaplane and the 1930s theme has been carefully and tastefully incorporated into the restaurant. Modern Scottish and British cuisines share the limelight with an impressive cocktail list.

Shropshire

This sparsely populated county sits on the border with Wales where locals enjoy a largely rural way of life with an abundance of open space, not least in the Shropshire Hills.

ABOVE Shropshire Blue cheese is just one of the varieties that the region is famous for.

RIGHT The Ludlow Food Festival attracts visitors from all over the country.

OPPOSITE The rolling hills of the Shropshire countryside.

Agriculture plays an important role in Shropshire life and this has historically always been a major farming region, with market towns, such as Shrewsbury and Market Drayton, providing the focal point for the local farming communities.

This glut of prime land has probably helped the area become a food destination. Rural communities have always been better at fending for themselves in culinary terms and small cottage industries would be born from necessity, becoming successful businesses as the word spread. The food of the region harks back to traditional farming days when hours spent in the fields were rewarded with hearty, filling meals: food that was tasty but never frivolous. Today's food lovers can expect much more, especially from award-winning restaurants and artisan producers, but the ethos of hard work and good, honest food remains unchanged.

Specialties and Local Producers

The county is known for its quality lamb and the traditional Shropshire breed is now being raised by an increasing number of farmers, keen to re-establish it. The area also has a number of breweries producing a vast range of ales making it one of the most important brewing regions in the country. Establishments such as the Three Tuns in

3 things you **must not** miss

◀ 1 Ludlow Food Festival
The highlight of the Shropshire foodie calendar takes place in September and draws visitors from all over the country. Regional food and drink producers gather to showcase their products. *www.foodfestival.co.uk*

2 Wroxeter Roman Vineyard
The idea of decent English wine used to be something of a joke but a number of wineries are now proving the doubters wrong. Wroxeter offers tours of its vineyard. *www.wroxetervineyard.co.uk*

3 Fair in the Square
This monthly fair in Shrewsbury town square gives local craftspeople, artisans and food producers the chance to sell their products directly to the public. *www.madein shropshire.co.uk*

Bishop's Castle have successfully carved out a niche as both brewery and restaurant. Ale has been brewed on the ancient site since the 17th century.

The specialties of Shropshire read like a ploughman's lunch, with ale and bread making a hefty contribution to the meal. However, no ploughman's would be complete without a large wedge of cheese and Shropshire doesn't disappoint on this count either. Award-winning Belton cheese has been made on the premises for hundreds of years, and the range includes a number of regional specialties and organic cheeses. Over at the Shropshire Cheese Company, varieties such as Marshes Blue and Smoked Tanatside have been making a name for themselves in culinary circles.

Markets and Shops

A county that delights in food to such an extent must surely provide plenty of opportunities for local producers to display and sell their products. Many Shropshire towns such as Ludlow, Shrewsbury and Bishop's Castle hold regular farmers' markets, while farm shops are dotted around the countryside. Moor Farm Shop near Baschurch stocks a wide variety of fresh vegetables, meat, eggs and home-made jams and Churncote Farm Shop in Shrewsbury is run from a cleverly converted cowshed, which also includes a butcher's counter.

For cheese fanatics, the Mousetrap has a shop in the center of Ludlow stocking a good range of local produce and some carefully selected continental varieties. Just down the road, the Marshes Little Beer Shoppe is also a champion of local products. The store is packed with local ale, cider and perry, along with a range of quirky and unusual beers from around the world. Also in Ludlow, De Grey's Bakery & Shop is a local favorite because customers know and appreciate that every loaf and cake is handmade and baked on the premises.

MR UNDERHILL'S
Dinham Weir
Ludlow SY8 1EH
t +44 1584 874431
w www.mr-underhills.co.uk

This superbly located eatery could easily rest on its laurels. Instead, the food more than lives up to its locale and there's a Michelin star to prove it.

THE INN AT GRINSHILL
High Street
Grinshill
SY4 3BL
t +44 1939 220410
w www.theinnat
    grinshill.co.uk

The delightful village setting could be straight from a chocolate box but the food goes way beyond façade. The modern European cuisine consistently gets rave reviews.

THE CLIVE BAR AND RESTAURANT
Bromfield
Ludlow
Shropshire SY8 2JR
t +44 1584 856565
w www.theclive.co.uk

The Clive serves modern British cuisine of the highest order but without the accompanying price tag, with sensibly priced wines. Immaculate bedrooms match the standards of the dining room, so you can always stay over if you've overindulged.

Monmouthshire

The Welsh county of Monmouthshire is located in the south-east of the country, with Monmouth, on the English border, its main town.

It's well worth visiting because there's an Area of Outstanding Natural Beauty, while Monmouth is an ancient settlement with plenty of architectural reminders of its past and, indeed, the whole county is steeped in history.

Despite its stunning natural resources and host of busy artisan producers, Wales has kept its culinary light largely hidden until now. While the locals have always known exactly where to buy the best bread, cheese, meat and fresh produce, the rest of Wales has been oblivious to the amazing foodstuffs in Monmouthshire. That is slowly changing and the reputation of the area is spreading. With towns such as Abergavenny carving out a culinary niche and first-rate restaurants opening up around the countryside it seems that Monmouthshire will finally get the credit it deserves as a bona-fide food destination.

Specialties and Local Producers

Tintern cheese gets its name from the village on the River Wye where you'll find Tintern Abbey. The cheese is produced by Abergavenny Fine Foods and is just one of their range of specialist Welsh cheeses. Wine might sound like a surprising addition to the Monmouthshire larder, yet the Sugarloaf Vineyards in the Brecon Beacons National Park is a thriving winery with a number of different grape varieties planted on this stunning site. Beer is also brewed in the county and Kingstone Brewery in

WHERE TO EAT

THE CROWN AT WHITEBROOK

Whitebrook, nr Monmouth
Monmouthshire NP25 4TX
t +44 1600 860254
w www.crownatwhite
   brook.co.uk

A Michelin-star restaurant with food that is a delectable combination of classic ingredients paired with unlikely surprises.

THE HARDWICK

Old Raglan Road
Abergavenny NP7 9AA
t +44 1873 854220
w www.thehardwick.co.uk

A country pub where head chef Stephen Terry has achieved the balance between classic and more ambitious dishes.

THE FOXHUNTER

Nantyderry, Abergavenny
Monmouthshire NP7 9DN
t +44 1873 881101
w www.thefoxhunter.com

Talented chef Matthew Tebbutt uses local produce to create modern British dishes that have excited the critics.

from Cefn Maen Farm in Raglan, also make regular appearances in farm shops and farmers' markets in the county.

Markets and Shops

There is a great variety of quality local produce, meat, cheese and other food and drinks at farmers' markets. Abergavenny and Monmouth both have excellent markets while there are plenty of farm shops that stock their own food, as well as selected goods from local suppliers. Meadow Farm in Tintern specializes in seasonal fruit and vegetables, as well as artisan bread and cheese.

The Tithe Barn in Abergavenny is a popular tourist attraction and features a food hall stocked with local delicacies while Deli Delicious is an upmarket food emporium in the town that sells freshly prepared sandwiches. For wonderful local beef and lamb head for H. J. Edwards & Son; Rawlings Family Butchers is an award-winning butcher that specializes in sausages offering a fantastic range of homemade varieties. Trealy Farm Charcuterie in Mitchel Troy has an unusual range of top-quality products, such as salami and chorizo. (Consult their website to see where you can buy their products.)

Tintern produce a range of award-winning ales based on traditional recipes.

Welsh beef and lamb is appreciated worldwide and has been given protected status to prove its worth. Pedigree sheep and cows are reared in farms all over Monmouthshire, and the quality and diversity of the meat is constantly evolving. The highest-quality wild game and free-range poultry, like the free-range turkeys

LEFT *Trealy Farm produces all manner of charcuterie, including chorizo and salami.*

OPPOSITE ABOVE *Local producers take pride in their unique sausage recipes.*

OPPOSITE BELOW *The Brecon Beacons National Park is a major tourist destination in Monmouthshire.*

3 things you must not miss

1 Abergavenny Food Festival

Cookery demonstrations and the best regional produce make this annual September event a firm favorite for locals and visitors alike. *www.abergavennyfood festival.com*

2 The Chef's Room Cookery School

A food writer and a chef have got together to create a series of cookery courses in state-of-the-art premises in Blaenavon. The school offers courses in everything from pasta to pastry and seafood preparation. *www.thechefsroom.co.uk*

▶ 3 Parva Farm Vineyard

Award-winning Welsh wine and mead is produced on this vineyard in Tintern. Visitors are welcome to look around, try some of the wines and visit the on-site shop. *www.parva farm.com*

London

In terms of the availability of ingredients, the abundance of restaurants and the choice of specialist shops and markets, it could easily be argued that London is the food capital of the UK.

ABOVE Square Pie has helped to spur on the London pie revolution.

RIGHT The London skyline is dotted with iconic buildings, including St. Paul's Cathedral.

OPPOSITE Borough Market is the biggest food market in the capital and one of the best known in the country.

Kent lies just to the south of the city and the aptly named "Garden of England" keeps London's many food markets and farm shops stocked with locally sourced produce. However, being a food destination isn't solely about the availability of quality ingredients. It is also about passion, innovation and pride, and London has these attributes in spades.

The diversity of the food and restaurants reflects the diversity of the population. It is possible to buy unusual ingredients from all over the world and to sample the cuisine of virtually any country you choose. Centuries of trade, travel and migration have resulted in a city with wonderfully eclectic taste buds and it's always keen to experiment. From single fruit stalls to cavernous market halls, from loose-change diners to Michelin-star restaurants, London is a food lover's paradise.

Specialties and Local Producers

Where to start? Meantime London is an award-winning brewery based in Greenwich, the artisan bakery Flour Power City has a fine reputation based on its

3 things you must not miss

◄ 1 Butchery Course at Ginger Pig
Learn the basics of meat preparation at this prestigious Marylebone butcher's. Choose from a number of hands-on courses. *www.thegingerpig.co.uk*

2 Taste of London
This annual food festival in Regent's Park has become a date in the diary for gastronomes. It offers the chance to sample food from many of the capital's top restaurants. *www.taste festivals.com/london*

3 Real Food Festival
Earl's Court is the venue for this dedicated real-food showcase, which demonstrates the popularity and importance of this culinary movement. *www.real foodfestival.co.uk*

range of bread and pastries and Square Pie has been instrumental in the recent pie revolution that has hit the streets of London. As Britain continues to experience a rise in the popularity of traditional dishes, pie shops have been springing up all over the capital. Pies are also firmly back on the menu in pubs and restaurants: there's even a Pie Club at the Windmill pub in Mayfair, for true aficionados.

Markets and Shops

You don't have to wander far in the capital to find a market or food emporium of some description. With over 8 million hungry Londoners to feed, food plays a vital role in city life. Borough Market is the obvious place to begin. This champion of quality British food is a treat for all the senses and you'll find everything from mouthwatering, sizzling game sausages and freshly baked bread to Spanish and Italian produce.

For Asian-inspired food, nowhere beats Brick Lane on Sunday. The area is steeped in the food and culture of the continent and the weekly market offers a dizzying array of street food, as well as authentic ingredients and produce. Fish lovers will be overwhelmed by the choice on offer at Billingsgate Market. The huge, noisy hall is packed with early-morning traders and porters, while restaurateurs and savvy locals rub their weary eyes and haggle over boxes of fish fresh from the boats. It might start at 5 a.m. but this is a "must-do" experience. For a more leisurely grocery shop, there are numerous farmers' markets dotted around London. They vary in size and frequency but all provide the opportunity to purchase food directly from farmers and producers. Blackheath, Notting Hill and Clapham are just a few of the weekly markets that have helped spark interest in locally sourced produce.

Discerning foodies also flock to the food halls at the more upmarket Fortnum & Mason, Harvey Nichols, Selfridges and Harrods for quality produce. For specialist food shopping, the options are endless. Cheese lovers line up at Neal's Yard Dairy in Covent Garden for a vast choice of British cheeses, while those with a sweet tooth head to one of the many world-renowned chocolatiers in the capital. William Curley and Paul A. Young are just two of the new generation encouraging a love of the genuine article.

WHERE TO EAT

❌❌❌
RESTAURANT GORDON RAMSAY
68 Royal Hospital Road
London SW3 4HP
t +44 20 73524441
w www.gordonramsay.
   com/royalhospitalroad

With three Michelin stars, this is the place to head to for top-quality dining in the capital. Superbly executed food in understated, immaculate surroundings.

❌❌
ST JOHN
26 St John Street
London EC1M 4AY
t +44 20 72510848
w www.stjohn
   restaurant.com

This is the restaurant that gave offal pride of place on the menu. It has a passion for what it terms "nose to tail eating," and the simply prepared dishes of quality food have attracted awards aplenty.

ANCHOR & HOPE
36 The Cut
London SE1 8LP
t +44 20 79289898

This Waterloo pub has been exciting customers and food critics for many years with its version of wholesome British cuisine. Stews and slow-roasted joints of meat are always popular, with many dishes designed for sharing.

Cornwall

Cornwall is now cited as one of the major food destinations in the UK, and with good reason.

ABOVE Cornish apples are good for eating, as well as for making cider.

RIGHT Most visitors will sample a cream tea during their stay in Cornwall.

OPPOSITE Padstow is one of the many picturesque fishing towns that are dotted around this seafaring county.

It is a region with two personalities. There is the public image of seaside resorts, stunning stretches of coastline and days spent eating pasties and ice cream. However, there is also hidden, rural Cornwall where farmers tend the land and remote communities remain relatively isolated. Recently, quality local food has come to the fore.

The abundance of fresh fish and seafood and quality seasonal produce and the prominence of artisan food producers have all helped put Cornwall on the gastronomic map. There are farm shops, orchards, tea rooms, bakers and cheese makers at every fork in the road, and a tour of the region will quickly yield some of the finest food that the UK has to offer.

Specialties and Local Producers

Cornwall is bursting at the seams with food and drink producers, many of whom

3 things you **must not** miss

◀ 1 Falmouth Oyster Festival
This annual party heralds the beginning of the oyster-dredging season. It's a celebration of all things seafood related and events include cookery demonstrations, live music and food stalls. *www.falmouth oysterfestival.co.uk*

2 Padstow
This fishing town is the jewel in the crown of Cornish gastronomy. There are a staggering number of quality eateries, as well as food shops and delicatessens. *www.padstow-cornwall.co.uk*

3 Cornwall Food and Drink Festival
This West Country festival gets bigger and better every year, and it showcases the best that Cornwall has to offer in terms of food and drink. The main events are in Truro but the whole county gets involved. *www.cornwallfood anddrinkfestival.com*

specialize in artisan products. The honey-flavored wine, mead, has been produced in Cornwall for centuries and local producers, such as Ninemaidens Mead, are now winning awards for their drinks. Cornwall is also well known for the quality of its cider and there are many independent cider farms catering to the growing demand.

With its lush, rolling hills Cornwall is ideally suited to dairy farming and where there are cows there is bound to be cheese. Cornish Blue is an award-winning, handmade cheese from the Cornish Cheese Co.'s farm in Liskeard and it's now popular all over the country. Cornish clotted cream is so synonymous with its place of origin that is has been awarded Protected Designation of Origin status, protecting it from poor imitations of this much-loved dairy product, which is an essential part of the cream tea. The prime fishing areas around the coast have also yielded a top-quality West Country product with a Protected Designation of Origin status. Cornish sardines (or scrowlers) are famed for their flavor and quality, and are a popular item on local restaurant menus.

Markets and Shops

Cornwall is justly proud of its gastronomic heritage, and the farmers' markets provide the perfect opportunity for local producers to showcase their wares. Larger towns, such as Truro and Falmouth, have their own weekly markets, while others run them on an ad hoc basis. There are also many farm shops offering a comparable selection of locally produced foods. Taste Cornwall in Liskeard is a shop run by the Cornish Guild of Smallholders, with everything on the shelves being produced in the area.

Cornish specialties can also be bought and tasted in more specific locations around the county, often on the premises where they are produced. If cider is your tipple of choice, the Cornish Cyder Farm in Penhallow offers a free tour of the press house and the opportunity to sample the cider before buying. For cheese lovers, the Cornish Farmhouse Cheese Shop in Penryn offers a comprehensive insight into the cheeses of the region. Another Cornish staple – ice cream – can be bought direct from the producers at Callestick Farm in Truro and Roskilly's in Helston.

WHERE TO EAT

● ● ● ● ● ● ● ● ● ● ● ● ●

✕✕✕
FIFTEEN
On the Beach
Watergate Bay
Cornwall TR8 4AA
t +44 1637 861000
w www.fifteencornwall.co.uk

Stunning sea views and an Italian-inspired menu greet customers at Jamie Oliver's West Country venue. With its trainee program for local youngsters keen to embark on a career in catering, this establishment has helped inject a new lease on life into an underrated area.

✕✕
OLD COASTGUARD HOTEL
Mousehole
Penzance
Cornwall TR19 6PR
t +44 1736 731222
w www.oldcoastguard
   hotel.co.uk

The food and views at this sensational seaside hotel and restaurant have bowled over the toughest critics.

✕
NEW YARD RESTAURANT
Trelowarren
Mawgan, Helston
Cornwall TR12 6AF
t +44 1326 221595
w www.newyard
   restaurant.co.uk

This informal restaurant on the beautiful Trelowarren estate sources almost all its ingredients locally. Food is freshly made on site and the wine list is renowned.

Fidget pie
SHROPSHIRE

serves **4–6**

4 Tbsp (50 g) butter

2 onions, thickly sliced

4 medium potatoes, peeled and finely sliced

2 cooking apples, peeled, cored and sliced

3 slices unsmoked ham

2 tsp brown sugar

½ tsp ground nutmeg

Salt and freshly ground black pepper

5 fl oz (150 ml) vegetable stock

9 oz (250 g) shortcrust pastry

Flour, for dusting

Beaten egg, to glaze

Preheat the oven to 350°F/180°C/gas mark 4.

Heat the butter in a large pan and sauté the onions, potatoes and apples until the onions have softened. Remove to a plate.

Place the ham in the pan and fry gently for 1–2 minutes. Transfer the ham to a 10in (1.5L) pie plate. Add the potato mixture, sugar and nutmeg, and season with salt and pepper. Stir gently to combine the ingredients, then gradually pour in the stock.

Roll out the pastry on a lightly floured surface and cover the pie. Trim the edges and make a steam hole in the center. Use the pastry trimmings to make decorations, and brush all over the pastry lid with beaten egg.

Bake the pie for 30 minutes and then check. The pie is ready when the pastry is golden brown. Cook for a further 10 minutes, if required.

Arbroath smokie pâté
ARBROATH

serves **4**

2 Arbroath smokies, skin and bones removed

5 fl oz (150 ml) crème fraiche

Juice of ½ lemon

1 Tbsp freshly chopped chives or finely sliced spring onion

Salt and freshly ground black pepper

Toast triangles or oatcakes, to serve

Place the Arbroath smokies in a large mixing bowl and fork through to create a rough textured paste. Alternatively, use a blender.

Add the crème fraiche, lemon juice and chives or spring onion and season with salt and pepper. Mix well to combine the ingredients.

Divide the mixture between four ramekins and place in the fridge to chill for 30 minutes. Serve with toast triangles or oatcakes.

IRELAND

WITH FARMING, FEUDALISM, famine and emigration all major parts of Ireland's history, it is easy to see why food has remained a constant source of comfort and pride over the years. The traditional dishes of the countryside traveled far and wide as people moved around the country and across the world. Now, however, the great quality of local producers is becoming much more widely known. There's a huge wave of interest in local foods, organic produce and Slow Food with visitors being treated to a plethora of farmhouse cheeses, cured fish and meat, fresh fish and seafood and some of the best restaurant food in Europe.

travel essentials

TIME ZONE: GMT

TELEPHONE CODE: +353

CURRENCY: Euro

CAPITAL: Dublin

LANGUAGE: English and Irish Gaelic

GETTING THERE: There are four international airports in Ireland – Dublin, Knock, Cork and Shannon – which cater to most of the regions. Two major bus companies offer services to the UK and mainland Europe, while bus travel within the country is also a popular means of getting about. Trains are limited with just a couple of services operating between Dublin and Belfast.

County Cork

The southwest of Ireland is a feast for all the senses. Besides being a particularly beautiful part of the country, it is the most important region for artisan food producers.

ABOVE Clonakilty black pudding is famous throughout Ireland and word is spreading even further afield.

RIGHT Despite the urban centers, County Cork is still very much a farming region.

OPPOSITE The Farmgate Cafe offers great views of the market hall below.

A disproportionate number of cheese, meat, fish and organic food producers live and work in Cork. Despite its lush natural resources and traditional culinary and farming heritage, Ireland took its time recognizing its homegrown talent and resources. However, County Cork has certainly made up for lost time. This area is prime food lover's territory with farm shops, artisan factories, festivals, tours and tastings at every turn. Use Cork city as a base to travel out to the likes of Clonakilty, Schull, Kinsale and other towns in the county that have earned a reputation as food destinations in their own right. Whatever you do, take your time – there's a lot of good food out there.

Specialties and Local Producers
County Cork is the artisan food larder of Ireland with new producers being attracted to the area and the greater range of products

3 things you must not miss

◀ 1 Ballymaloe House and Cookery School
This unique and highly regarded cookery school is located on a 100-acre organic farm. Ballymaloe has become a byword for quality Irish food.
www.cookingisfun.ie

2 Slow Food Cork Summer Picnic
Join the locals as they climb to the top of a hill and enjoy the view while tucking into a specially prepared picnic that highlights the best that local producers have to offer.
www.slowfoodireland.com

3 Cork Coastal Food Trail
Take a self-guided tour and explore the region's gastronomy. Gorgeous scenery combines with mouthwatering food.
www.discoverireland.ie/ food/Food-Trails.aspx

encouraging even more visitors. Sally Barnes is something of a legend and her Woodcock Smokery in Castletownshend uses wild, locally caught fish to make some of the best smoked haddock, mackerel and salmon you will ever taste. The smokehouse Ummera in Inchybridge was set up by a fisherman and is now run by his son, and features salmon, eel, chicken, bacon and duck.

Timoleague brown pudding and Clonakilty black pudding are both revered, with their puddings prepared to traditional recipes that are sold all over the country. The variety of local cheeses has exploded in Ireland over the last few years and this is largely thanks to the cottage industries in Cork, where a number of quality varieties are produced. They include the delicate cow's milk cheese, Milleens, which can claim to be the first farmhouse cheese to be produced in Cork. Other cheese producers include Ardrahan and Durrus.

Markets and Shops

Farmers' markets have no shortage of goods to sell or people to buy them.

Clonakility Market is held every Friday and offers a great selection of local food. The Saturday farmers' market in Skibbereen is laden down with produce, cheeses, meats and preserves, and the Dingle Farm Produce and Craft Market specializes in seafood and smoked fish, as well as handmade crafts and artisan food products. Princes Street Market in Cork city center has been selling produce since the 18th century and the Farmgate Cafe above the main trading hall has become the in-place to go once the shopping is done.

If you want to swap market stalls for shelves, Nash 19 in the city center offers that ideal combination of a shop and restaurant. In Bantry, Mannings Emporium supplies everything the aspiring gourmand needs to rustle up a meal. There is an extensive range of Cork cheeses and other local foods, as well as international brands of note. For quality meat prepared in the traditional way, Frank Murphy Butchers in Midleton is the place. For a wide range of local specialties and black and white puddings head to Staunton's in Timoleague.

WHERE TO EAT

● ● ● ● ● ● ● ● ● ● ● ● ● ● ●

✖✖✖
ISLAND COTTAGE
Heir Island
Skibbereen
West Cork
t +353 28 38102
w www.islandcottage.com

This highly unusual island restaurant is only open for dinner from June to September. There's a set menu that changes daily. It's like going to someone's house for top-quality restaurant food.

✖✖
CAFÉ PARADISO
16 Lancaster Quay
Cork City
t +353 21 4277939
w www.cafeparadiso.ie

Something of a Cork institution and one of the most famous vegetarian restaurants in the country. The elegant dining space shows off the stunning food at its best and chef Denis Cotter has earned the restaurant a number of prestigious awards.

✖
THE CUSTOMS HOUSE
Baltimore
Co. Cork
t +343 28 20200

Fish is the specialty, with daily menus chalked up on the blackboard. It's a sophisticated eatery serving classic fish and meat dishes with a unique flair.

Dublin

The capital of Ireland, with a compact city center, lies midway up Ireland's east coast. The city's cuisine has evolved enormously during recent times, but it hasn't lost its identity.

In fact the classic dishes of the city and the country have found new fame in the contemporary cafes and restaurants of the capital. Dublin wears its heart on its sleeve and although there is plenty to tempt the Michelin-savvy diner, there is also a great deal of individuality and creativity in mainstream eateries.

Specialties and Local Producers

Seafood is popular all over the country and there is plenty of opportunity to try out the freshest and best-quality lobster, prawns and fish in the capital. Dublin Bay prawns, though not actually caught in the bay, are known elsewhere as langoustines. Incredibly succulent,

WHERE TO EAT

⊗⊗⊗

RESTAURANT PATRICK GUILBAUD

21 Upper Merrion Street
Dublin 2
t +353 1 6764192
w www.restaurantpatrick
guilbaud.ie

The place for the ultimate in fine dining. Holding two Michelin stars, the quality is second-to-none.

⊗⊗

WINDING STAIR

40 Ormond Quay
Dublin 1
t +353 1 8727320
w www.winding-stair.com

This highly praised restaurant has a menu of delicious Irish food veering towards the organic.

⊗

AVOCA CAFÉ

11–13 Suffolk Street
Dublin 2
t +353 1 672 6019
w www.avoca.ie

Avoca is known to every Dubliner. This famous mini department store's cafe is perfect for cakes and sandwiches, and for soaking up a real piece of Dublin history.

3 things you **must not** miss

1 The Kitchen in the Castle Cookery School
The school is based in the stunning Howth Castle, offering courses on an endless range of skills and cuisines, for every level of cook. *www.thekitcheninthe castle.com*

2 Taste of Dublin
A gourmet fair held each June that is a treasure trove of demonstrations, restaurant visits, sampling and tasting. Don't miss it. *www.tasteof dublin.ie*

▶ 3 Guinness Storehouse
This tour features the history and production of Ireland's famous export and has become the most popular attraction in the city. It's a fascinating, fun exploration of the noble brew, culminating in a pint in the bar with great views over the city.
www.guinness-storehouse.com

they are typically served with a simple butter sauce, sometimes with a touch of garlic, to ensure the main ingredient shines. A favorite lobster recipe is Dublin Lawyer, a decadent dish prepared with cream and Irish whiskey. Another traditional dish is Dublin coddle (see page 142), a kind of layered stew of bacon, sausages, onions and potatoes.

Markets and Shops

Farming has always had an important role to play in the economy and social history of Ireland. With the renewed interest in artisan foods, there have been greater opportunities for producers and customers to meet. The Dublin Food Co-op is a twice-weekly shop-cum-market featuring some of the best locally produced food including cheese, meat, deli produce, fresh fruit and vegetables. There are a couple of CoCo Farmers' Markets in Dublin that also feature local producers, as well as international food and gourmet items. Ballymun Farmers' Market runs every Thursday and the Saturday Temple Bar Food Markets are a city-center favorite.

Fallon & Byrne Food Hall is a giant gourmet "supermarket," a one-stop shop for the best of the best. Meat, fish, cheese, pickles, charcuterie, cakes and biscuits – it's all here. And if you fancy a night away from the oven, The Gallic Kitchen will do all the hard work for you. The homemade pies, quiches and tarts are enough to tempt anyone out of the kitchen. Finally, the Avoca shop should be on everybody's list with its incredible range of gourmet treats and quality kitchenware.

OPPOSITE ABOVE Seafood, such as lobster, features widely on Dublin restaurant menus.

OPPOSITE BELOW The River Liffey runs through the center of Dublin and buildings such as the Four Courts line its banks.

BELOW Temple Bar Food Market is a popular Saturday shopping destination for Dubliners.

Baked trout with champ

IRISH CLASSIC

serves 2

2 x 5 oz (150 g) trout fillets
Salt and freshly ground black pepper
1 Tbsp (15 g) butter
½ lemon
Handful of chopped parsley

FOR THE CHAMP:
2 large potatoes, peeled and diced
2 oz (50 g) chopped scallions
¼ cup (50 ml) milk
2 Tbsp (25 g) butter, plus extra to serve
Salt and freshly ground black pepper

Preheat the oven to 340°F/170°C/gas mark 3–4.

Place the trout fillets in the center of a large sheet of aluminum foil and season with salt and pepper. Place a knob of butter on each fillet and squeeze a little lemon juice on top. Raise up the sides of the foil to create a parcel and seal on top, leaving space for the steam. Place the parcel on a cookie sheet and cook in the oven for 15–20 minutes, or until cooked through.

Meanwhile, boil the potatoes in salted water for 20 minutes. Cook the scallions in the milk for about 5 minutes. Drain the potatoes well, return to the pan and pour in the milk and onions. Add the butter, season with salt and pepper, and mash the potatoes until creamy.

Place a mound of champ in the center of each plate and finish with the extra butter. Carefully place the trout fillet on top, sprinkle with parsley and serve immediately.

Dublin coddle

DUBLIN

serves 4–6

1 Tbsp vegetable oil
9 oz (250 g) smoked streaky bacon, sliced
8 good-quality sausages
2 medium onions, sliced
8 large potatoes, peeled and cut into quarters
18 fl oz (500 ml) vegetable stock or water
2 Tbsp freshly chopped parsley, to serve
Soda bread, to serve

Heat the oil in a large frying pan and brown the bacon and sausages for about 5 minutes. Remove the meat from the pan and cut the sausages into three pieces. Add the onions to the pan and soften in the meat fat for 1–2 minutes.

Beginning with potato, arrange layers of potato, onion and meat in a large casserole dish that is safe to be used on your stovetop. Repeat for three layers and finish with a final layer of potato. Carefully pour the stock into the dish and bring to the boil.

Reduce the heat to a simmer, cover the dish and then simmer for about 1 hour, until the potatoes are tender. Sprinkle chopped parsley on top and serve with soda bread.

DENMARK

DENMARK AND ITS islands lie to the north of Germany, reaching out into the North Sea, receiving shelter from the west of Sweden. In fact apart from its German border, the country is surrounded by water. With its Viking history, Denmark marked itself out as an adventurous and independently-minded nation and this trait has continued to the present, with the country being one of the founding members of both the UN and NATO.

Denmark also learned to be self-sufficient from the earliest times, growing vegetables and cereals. That's still the case, with recipes from the past playing an important role. Hearty stews to combat cold winters, sausages, salami, rye bread and, of course, herring make up the mainstay of the national cuisine. However, new influences are slowly infiltrating and there are exciting times ahead as more experimental young chefs conjure up modern interpretations of traditional Danish fare.

travel essentials

TIME ZONE: **GMT +1**

TELEPHONE CODE: **+45**

CURRENCY: **Danish Krone**

CAPITAL: **Copenhagen**

LANGUAGE: **Danish**

GETTING THERE: The two main airports in the country are Copenhagen and Billund, and you are likely to land at one of these, although some of the budget airlines fly solely into smaller, regional airports. A good train service also operates to Copenhagen or Jutland from Hamburg. Part of the journey is by ferry but it only takes a matter of hours. It is possible to drive directly from Germany.

Copenhagen

With a growing number of Michelin-starred restaurants, the city has attracted attention with its new wave of Danish cuisine and classic dishes being given a modern makeover by experimental chefs.

ABOVE Coffee is taken extremely seriously at Coffee Collective.

RIGHT Noma demonstrates the successful Danish blend of tradition and modernity.

OPPOSITE Lagkagehuset is just one of the many outstanding bakeries in the city center.

Copenhagen lies mostly on the east coast of the island of Zealand, which means that it is geographically closer to Sweden than to much of Denmark. It has its own culture, cuisine and lifestyle and is a lively city while it eschews some of the baggage affecting other capital cities. Copenhagen has also embraced environmentalism and adopted a greener lifestyle with the bicycle now more popular than the car. In addition, the city is rapidly becoming known for its fine food.

3 things you **must not** miss

◄ 1 Copenhagen Cooking
From rustic country cooking to innovative creations, this 10-day long festival celebrates all things Danish.
www.copenhagencooking.dk

2 Coffee Tasting at Coffee Collective
This micro-roastery aims to give customers the best coffee on the planet. It runs a series of talks and tastings for those with a nose for beans.
www.coffeecollective.dk

3 Copenhagen Beer Festival
This popular spring festival offers visitors the chance to sample some of the finest beers in the country over a period of three days.
www.visitcopenhagen.com

Specialties and Local Producers

Copenhagen is known for its incredible open sandwiches that can be bought from food stalls, cafes or high-end eateries. The bread of choice is generally rye bread, and fillings are often a delicate and carefully orchestrated combination of flavors and ingredients designed to deliver the ultimate taste sensation. The regular sight of sausage wagons (*pølsevogn*) is also guaranteed to whet the appetite. Essentially a hot dog, these sausages are given an extra lift with the addition of the typical Danish sauce, *remoulade*.

Historically, pickling, curing and smoking were essential preparation methods that ensured that food supplies remained constant during lean winter months. They have since become synonymous with the food of the region and dishes such as *gravad laks* have found international appreciation, while pickled herrings and cucumbers are popular sandwich toppings. Beer remains the most popular drink in Copenhagen to accompany a meal and with such a top-notch brewing pedigree this is no great surprise. Carlsberg is the big name in the city but there are over 50 breweries in and around Copenhagen, including a number of microbreweries where you can enjoy the beer on tap.

Markets and Shops

Coffee is a national obsession and there are plenty of places to sample and buy some of the best blends. Estate Coffee and Coffee Collective are just two big names to look out for. Cities with an established coffee culture usually have a penchant for cakes and pastries, and Copenhagen is no exception. Award-

winning bakeries line the streets and the aromas of fresh batches of bread, cakes and biscuits are hard to ignore. Lagkagehuset bakery is one of the best, and Reinh van Hauen is the place to buy the classic Danish pastry.

The upmarket department store Magasin du Nord supplies all the ingredients for a gourmet dinner. The basement of this famous shop is stocked full of great food and drink, and includes a fancy delicatessen called Meyer's, which also serves food. If you want to experience open sandwiches at their best, head to Aamanns for a beautiful takeaway box. Or, if you'd rather try and create your own sandwiches, a trip to Östermalms Saluhall indoor food market is obligatory.

WHERE TO EAT

NOMA
Strandgade 93
1401 Copenhagen K
t +45 3296 3297
w www.noma.dk

Noma combines the traditions of Nordic cuisine with an artistic contemporary flair. Age-old cooking techniques are used to create elegant food served in a cool minimalist interior.

THE PAUL
Vesterbrogade 3 (Tivoli Gardens)
Copenhagen 1630
t +45 3375 0775
w www.thepaul.dk

Chef Paul Cunningham shows off his passion for food with this delightfully unfussy menu of classic flavors and locally sourced food.

SAA HVIDT
Snaregade 4
Copenhagen 1205 K
t +45 3391 0191
w www.saahvidt.dk

This diminutive downtown eatery offers traditional Danish dishes that have been sympathetically updated to reflect contemporary Danish cuisine. Excellent value and quality.

Danish meatballs

Frikadeller

DANISH CLASSIC

serves **4**

2 slices white bread, no crust

1¼ cups (300 ml) whole milk

1 lb (450 g) ground veal or lamb

1 Tbsp salt

1 large onion, grated

1 clove garlic

½ tsp finely chopped thyme

1 large egg

Salt and freshly ground black pepper

1 Tbsp (15 g) butter

Flour, for dusting

Boiled potatoes and gravy, to serve

Put the bread into a bowl, add the milk and let it soak for 10 minutes.

Put the remaining ingredients, except the butter and flour, in a separate, large mixing bowl and mix together well. Drain the bread, then add to the mixture and combine.

Dust some flour onto a large plate. Take tablespoons of the meat mixture and form into neat balls, then place on the plate. Repeat until all the mixture is used. Cover the meatballs with plastic wrap and chill in the fridge for 30 minutes.

Melt the butter in a large frying pan then add the meatballs in batches. Fry the meatballs over a medium heat until golden brown and until the meat is cooked through. Serve with boiled potatoes and gravy.

NORWAY

THIS SCANDINAVIAN COUNTRY is one of the least populated in Europe but what it lacks in numbers it makes up for in activity. The population is known for its love of the great outdoors and the multitude of fjords, islands, forests and mountains provide ample playgrounds. This outdoor lifestyle is reflected in the food and its preparation. As a result of its extensive coastline, fish is a major part of the diet, especially smoked salmon. Hunting game is another major pursuit.

travel essentials

TIME ZONE: GMT +1

TELEPHONE CODE: +47

CURRENCY: Norwegian Krone

CAPITAL: Oslo

LANGUAGE: Norwegian

GETTING THERE: There is a good train service between Norway and its neighboring countries. There are a number of airports, including Sandefjord, Oslo and Stavanger, all of which operate international services. Planes are often used for internal travel. Ferries sail between Norway and Germany, Denmark and England, among other destinations.

Oslo

Oslo might be the capital city of Norway but its numerous large parks and green spaces give it a much more rural feel, while it's only a short distance from the forests.

ABOVE Cinnamon buns are just one of many sweet treats available in Oslo cafes.

RIGHT Oslo has a sense of calm and space and it's easy to escape city life.

OPPOSITE Fishing is a popular pastime and it's also possible to buy seafood direct from fishermen.

3 things you **must not** miss

◀ 1 Aker Brygge
The marina area of the city is a great place to explore, soak up the atmosphere and dine. A wide choice of restaurants, many specializing in shrimp and other seafood.
www.akerbrygge.no

2 Matstreif
This annual event draws producers from around the region. Plenty of fresh produce and traditional food products to taste and buy.
www.innovasjonnorge.no/Pro sjekter/Matstreif/

3 Fjord Fishing
Oslo fjord is a popular venue. The islands and beaches are popular with locals and tourists, and fjord fishing makes a great day out.
www.visitnorway.com/en/ product/?pid=44951

When city life becomes too constrictive it is simple enough to escape and achieve a sense of space and freedom, either within the city itself or just outside. The city has plenty of sights and attractions, including the Kon-Tiki Museum and the Viking Ship Museum, which highlight the achievements of Norwegians and showcase the ancient history and culture of this Scandinavian country.

Oslo has become more culturally diverse over recent years, which is evident in its eating habits that now encompass a number of influences. So while typical Norwegian restaurants sit happily beside eateries from all over the world, the locals have learned more than ever to appreciate the finer aspects of their traditional cuisine.

Specialties and Local Producers

Oslo might have welcomed fast-food joints and snack bars into its environs with open arms, but the locals were hardly strangers to the notion of grabbing a quick bite to eat on the run before these establishments arrived en masse. The inhabitants are partial to *pølse*, a boiled sausage that is served in a bun and sold from snack wagons all over the city. Other Norwegian specialties include *spekemat*, a type of traditional dried meat that was an essential part of the larder when times were lean and fresh meat was at a premium. Today, it is a popular delicacy sharing top billing with *fenalår*, a cured leg of mutton that is served in thin slices. The Norwegians aren't shy about using every bit of the animal and another specialty on Oslo menus is *smalahove*, a boiled, salted sheep's head, traditionally served around Christmas.

Vodka and beer are the usual tipples at dinner and Oslo has the largest brewery in the country, Ringnes, which produces a range of drinks that are popular in the city and beyond. There are also a number of microbreweries and brewpubs dotted around the city, with Oslo Mikrobryggeri being one of the most respected with its selection of stout, ale and bitter.

Markets and Shops

Oslo is a fantastic place for gourmet window-shoppers and serious buyers. There is a selection of markets, including Vibesgate Farmers' Market, selling the best regional produce. The Paleet Shopping Center is a major attraction and has a gorgeous food court when it's time for lunch. More dining options can be found in the trendy Aker Brygge area of the city, where there's a huge selection of restaurants.

Fenaknoken is a delicatessen offering local delicacies, such as cured meat, smoked salmon, cheese and beer, which will have gourmands salivating. Gutta på Haugen gives its more famous neighbor a run for its money with its homely layout and abundance of favorite deli items, and Pascal Konditori is the place to buy pastries, confectionery and jams.

WHERE TO EAT

⊗⊗⊗
STATHOLDERGAARDEN
Rådhusgate 11
Kirkegaten
0151 Oslo
t +47 22 41 88 00
w www.statholder
gaarden.no

The beautiful dining room and creative menu have made this restaurant a popular spot for high-end eating. Head chef Bent Stiansen has previously won the prestigious Bocuse d'Or competiton, and it shows.

⊗⊗
BØLGEN & MOI
1311 Hovikodden
Onstad Kunstsenter
Høvikodden
Oslo
t +47 67 52 10 20
w www.bolgenogmoi.no

This smart eatery is a bit off the beaten track, so it's no tourist trap. There are options for different numbers of courses and a pizzeria for a more informal meal.

⊗
STORTORVETS GJÆSTGIVERI
Grensen 1
0159 Oslo
t +47 23 35 63 60
w www.stortorvets-
gjestgiveri.no

One of the city's oldest restaurants with traditional Norwegian food and impeccable service.

Seafood bisque

Fiskesuppe

NORWEGIAN CLASSIC

serves **4–6**

1 Tbsp olive oil

1 medium onion, finely chopped

1 small leek, trimmed and thinly sliced

3½ cups (1 L) fish stock

2 medium potatoes, peeled and diced

3 fl oz (75 ml) white wine

24 raw shrimp, peeled

1 salmon fillet, about 5 oz (150 g)

1 cod fillet, about 5 oz (150 g)

Handful freshly chopped parsley

⅔ cup (150 ml) half and half

⅔ cup (150 ml) sour cream

Salt and freshly ground black pepper

Heat the oil in a large pan and fry the onion and leek for about 5 minutes, until softened. Pour the stock into the pan, add the potatoes and bring back to the boil, then reduce to a simmer.

Add the wine, shrimp, salmon and cod to the pan, bring back to a simmer and cook for about 5–7 minutes, until the fish begins to look flaky.

Add half the parsley, cook for 1–2 minutes then add the half and half and sour cream and season with salt and pepper. Stir and cook for a further 2 minutes, then remove the pan from the heat. Transfer the bisque to serving bowls and garnish with the remaining parsley.

SWEDEN

SWEDEN BORDERS NORWAY on the west, Finland on the north and the Baltic Sea lies along its east coast. It's a vast country with much of the north covered in forest and the main population concentrated in the south. Large lakes and national parks, coupled with the huge tracts of agricultural land, lend a rural feel to the country and yet the urban areas are decidedly modern. Sweden enjoys a high standard of living.

The traditional food is sturdy and filling. Temperatures can plummet during winter and big, hearty plates of food are a traditional necessity. A classic dish of meatballs and mashed potatoes sums up the Swedish dinner table, although there is far more to it than meat and vegetables. Wild berries are made into jams, fermented herring tests the palate of the most hardened foodie while mushroom foraging is popular in the autumn.

travel essentials

TIME ZONE: GMT +1

TELEPHONE CODE: +46

CURRENCY: Swedish Krona

CAPITAL: Stockholm

LANGUAGE: Swedish

GETTING THERE: The two main airports are Stockholm and Gothenburg, although a number of smaller airports, used by budget airlines, also offer flights to, and from, neighboring countries. Trains frequently run between the Scandinavian countries. Train travel is the recommended mode of transport within Sweden itself. Boat services operate to a number of countries.

Stockholm

The fascinating city of Stockholm consists of a series of 14 islands, with the larger metropolitan area extending onto the mainland.

ABOVE Kanelbullar *are the Swedish version of cinnamon buns and they're a popular sweet treat.*

OPPOSITE ABOVE Fermented *herring (*surströmming*) is not to everyone's taste.*

OPPOSITE BELOW Stockholm is *a picturesque city that never feels too cramped or frenetic.*

The sense of openness is highlighted by the huge number of parks and the constant interruption of water that helps break up the urban environment. Stockholm is relaxed and dynamic in equal measures, just like its cuisine.

There are many similarities between the food of Stockholm and the rest of the country and, indeed, Scandinavia. Pickling and other methods of preserving food were traditional ways of guaranteeing food supplies during the long winter months, before fridges were commonplace. These traditional practices are still popular, and cured meats and fish remain an important part of the culture. Bread and potatoes are staple foods, vodka warms up chilly dark winter evenings and coffee is consumed by the bucketful.

Specialties and Local Producers

Stockholm is the perfect place to try some particularly Swedish specialties.

Surströmming is an acquired taste, and for many one helping is quite enough. These cans of fermented herring have a pungent smell and should only be opened outside as the rotting fish can cause them to virtually explode. Crayfish have a wider appeal and when crayfish season gets under way in August, these delectable shellfish are consumed in great quantities at lively gatherings (*kräftskiva*) all over the capital.

Salmon is another Stockholm staple, and the simple preparation of cured salmon called *gravad lax* (see page 154) is served on crispbread as a snack or light meal. When something hearty is called for, meatballs (*köttbullar*) are the first choice; they are usually served with a generous helping of potatoes and gravy with another specialty, lingonberry jam. Coffee is another essential, and is often accompanied by a cake or biscuit. Also look out for *kanelbullar*, a delicious cinnamon bun.

3 things you **must not** miss

◀ **1 Taste of Stockholm**
The annual five-day June festival is a major event on the Stockholm calendar. Local food and drink is consumed to the backdrop of live entertainment. *www.smakapa stockholm.se*

2 Hotel Rival
This contemporary hotel complex includes an art-house cinema, bakery, bar, bistro and restaurant, all on one site. It's a great place to sample the best local cuisine. *www.rival.se*

3 Skansen
Discover Sweden past in this impressive open-air museum, which features traditional houses and craftspeople demonstrating traditional skills, such as bookbinding and baking. *www.skansen.se*

Markets and Shops

The best Stockholm market is the Östermalms Saluhall Indoor Market. The hall is a masterpiece of quality and creativity and some would argue that there is little point in shopping anywhere else. But there is certainly more to be seen and that doesn't mean more of the same. Kista Food Court contains an enormous collection of eateries offering every possible type of food under one roof, while Street is a bustling weekly market in Södermalm. It specializes in clothing and crafts but is surrounded by numerous cafes and restaurants.

Back indoors Cajsa Warg is a foodie gem that stocks top-quality delicatessen products and offers the option of ordering ready-packed picnic baskets from a choice of menus. The food hall in the

famous NK department store is another treasure trove packed with exclusive products and unusual local specialties, and Aubergine specializes in organic produce and ingredients.

WHERE TO EAT

. . . .

✖✖✖
B.A.R
Blasieholmsgatan 4A
111 48 Stockholm
t +46 8 611 53 35
w www.restaurangbar.se

"The simplicity of the sea" is the catchphrase of the veteran restaurateurs Henrik Norström and Peter Johansson. The food is based around the freshest ingredients and the menu injects some international flavor into typical Swedish dishes.

✖✖
STUREHOF AB
Sturegallerian 42
Stureplan 2
114 46 Stockholm
t +46 8 440 57 30
w www.sturehof.com

The seafood is the main attraction but the wine list follows a close second and is one of the best lists in Stockholm. Traditional Swedish cuisine in a smart dining room with bars where you can lounge after dinner.

✖
KOFI
Birger Jarlsgatan 11
Stockholm
t +46 8 611 33 35
w www.kofi.se

There is nothing flashy about this popular, local delicatessen-cum-cafe. The unpretentious decor and relaxed atmosphere make coffee and bagels a real pleasure.

Cured salmon

Gravad lax

SWEDISH CLASSIC

serves 6

1½ lbs (700 g) salmon fillet (skin on)

1½ Tbsp (25 g) sea salt

½ tsp freshly ground white pepper

½ cup (50 g) roughly chopped fresh dill

½ cup (100 g) granulated sugar

Trim the salmon of fat and use tweezers to remove any bones.

In a large bowl, mix together the salt, pepper, dill and sugar.

Spread a layer of plastic wrap in the bottom of a shallow dish. Place the salmon on top of the plastic wrap, skin-side down. Spread the sugar and salt mix over the salmon and rub it in thoroughly.

Wrap the plastic wrap tightly around the salmon. Place a heavy cutting board or flat plate on top of the salmon and weigh this down with cans or a brick, and then place in the fridge for 24 hours.

Pour off any liquid from the dish and turn the salmon over. Weigh it down again and return to the fridge for another 24 hours. The *gravad lax* is now ready but will keep for another five days if left unsliced.

FINLAND

FINLAND IS A large, sparsely populated country in northern Europe. It is bordered by Russia, Norway and Sweden while its western territory overlooks the Baltic Sea. Like its immediate Nordic neighbors, a large percentage of the landscape (in this case, three-quarters) is covered by forest. The country is also punctuated by thousands of lakes, giving it a rather beautiful and remote feel, with water and forest often stretching away as far as the eye can see with no hint of human life. Fish, game and milk are key components of the Finnish diet, as they are in the rest of the Nordic region. Smoked and pickled fish are widely consumed and regional specialties, such as Karelian pasties (see page 158) and sautéed reindeer, have become national favorites.

travel essentials

TIME ZONE: GMT +2
TELEPHONE CODE: +358
CURRENCY: Euro
CAPITAL: Helsinki
LANGUAGE: Finnish

GETTING THERE: Helsinki-Vantaa is the main airport with plenty of international flights. Traveling by sea is a popular way to arrive in Finland, and journeys on the massive boats from Sweden are as much social events as transport. It is also possible to travel cheaply between Russia and Finland by bus and train.

Helsinki

Helsinki clearly respects its traditions but is happy to embrace the best offerings from modern chefs, and fusion cuisine has found a new, receptive audience.

ABOVE Berries are easy to find and foraging is a popular pastime throughout Finland.

OPPOSITE ABOVE The Wanha Kauppahalli (Old Market Hall) is a popular spot for coffee and cake.

OPPOSITE BELOW Mushrooms are another popular ingredient for foragers to search out.

The capital city of Finland sits on the southern edge of the long, teardrop-shaped country, just across the Gulf of Finland from Estonia. Helsinki covers a wide geographical area that spans a number of islands, waterways and peninsulas, many with a very distinctive feel. The city is influenced by the rest of the country, which is largely divided into two regions, the east and west. Helsinki gets the best of both worlds, enjoying the dense, hearty meat dishes, the wide variety of smoked fish, the hearty pasties and stews and the wonderful selection of regional breads that play an important part in the Finnish diet.

Specialties and Local Producers

As a collective set of islands forming the country's capital city, Helsinki has a rich supply of fresh fish. Many regional specialties are based on fish and seafood, and both fresh and smoked fish have an equal place on the menu.

Hunting is a passionate pastime in many parts of the country and marketplaces are the best venues to purchase delicious fresh reindeer meat (*poronliha*). This love of the wild extends to foraging and Finland is famous for its profusion of wild mushrooms and berries, many of which have made their way into everyday and restaurant meals. Foraging for lingonberries, cranberries, chanterelles, etc. is at its most fervent between July and October. Experienced foragers stock up their winter cupboards with these wonderful and abundant ingredients.

Beer and vodka have always been the favored traditional drinks in Helsinki, and there is now a return to small-scale brewing with new companies producing highly rated artisan beers. Downtown Brewery Ltd is one such brewer with a selection of drinks, including some sahti beers. These fermented beers have a distinct banana flavor and a cloudy appearance.

3 things you **must not** miss

◀ 1 Baltic Herring Festival
This October celebration of the famous fish brings the Market Square alive. Fishermen, stallholders and herring fans gather together to appreciate this national treasure. *www.visithelsinki.fi*

2 Helsinki Beer Festival
Enjoy a selection of local brews to the accompaniment of live music at this annual April festival. *www.helsinki beerfestival.com*

3 Fishing
Why buy your fish at the market when you can hire a boat and catch your own supper in the heart of the city? *www.fishingin helsinki.com*

Markets and Shops

There are markets galore in Helsinki and they offer the chance to buy some products that aren't readily available in supermarkets, such as foraged foods and wild meat. The Market Square (Kauppatori) is by far the best known and this central marketplace will take care of all your grocery needs. There is also a fish market here where you can buy cured fish. Hakaniemi Market Hall is a vast food hall that benefits from being undercover on colder days, and Hietalahti Market Hall is the place to go for organic produce.

Sis. Deli & Café is a wonderfully modern food outlet where raw ingredients or prepared salads and soups can be bought for a quick snack while Tokyokan is the place to buy Japanese food and tableware. Sushi is very popular in Helsinki, and you'll have no trouble buying everything you need to create your own dishes.

WHERE TO EAT

CHEZ DOMINIQUE
Rikhardinkatu 4
00130 Helsinki
t +358 9 612 7393
w www.chezdominique.fi

This beautiful restaurant takes food to another level with its eclectic combination of Nordic and French flavors. The awards have flooded in, including two Michelin stars.

POSTRES
Eteläesplanadi 8
Helsinki
t +358 9 663 300
w www.postres.fi

Postres has been grabbing the headlines here and abroad with its modern flair for Finnish food. A variety of menus is available with twists and surprises in every course.

KOLME KRUUNUA
Liisankatu 5
00170 Helsinki
t +358 9 135 4172
w www.kolmekruunua.fi

The decor has changed little since the 1950s when this iconic Helsinki eatery opened its doors. The food is gutsy Finnish fare, and includes meatballs and reindeer. As authentic as anything you'll find in the city.

Karelian rice pasties

Karjalanpiirakat

KARELIA

makes **15**

4 cups (400 g) rye flour
½ tsp salt
¾ cup (180 ml) water

FOR THE FILLING:
1¼ cups (300 ml) water
¾ cup (150 g) white rice
1 pt (600 ml) milk
Salt

To make the filling, bring the water to the boil in a large saucepan. Add the rice, stir then reduce the heat to a simmer and cook, uncovered, for about 10 minutes, until most of the water is absorbed.

Add the milk to the pan and stir to combine. Reduce the heat again and simmer for 10–15 minutes, until the milk has been absorbed and the rice resembles a thick rice pudding. Remove the pan from the heat, season with salt and set aside to cool.

Preheat the oven to 450°F/230°C/gas mark 8. Line one large or two small baking pans with wax paper.

Mix the flour and salt together in a large mixing bowl, then add the water and mix again to form a dough. Divide into 15 balls and flatten each one into a thin circle shape.

Divide the filling between the circles leaving a thick border. Fold the borders in towards the center to make a ridge around the edge but leave the filling exposed. Place in the baking pans and cook in the oven for about 10 minutes, until golden brown.

TOURIST INFORMATION WEBSITES

Austria www.austria.info

Bulgaria www.bulgariatravel.org

Croatia www.croatia.hr

Czech Republic www.czechtourism.com

Denmark www.denmark.dk

Estonia www.visitestonia.com

Finland www.visitfinland.com

France www.francetourism.com

Germany www.germany-tourism.de

Greece www.gnto.gr

Hungary www.budapestinfo.hu

Ireland www.visitbritain.com

Italy www.italiantourism.com

Lithuania www.visitlithuania.net

Netherlands www.holland.com

Norway www.visitnorway.com

Poland www.poland.travel

Portugal www.visitportugal.com

Romania www.romaniatourism.com

Slovakia www.slovakia.travel

Spain www.spain.info

Sweden www.visitsweden.com

Turkey www.tourismturkey.org

United Kingdom www.visitbritain.com

PICTURE CREDITS

(Wayra), 89 (Martin Dimintrov), 90 (Fotozonas), 92 top left (TravellingLight), 92 bottom right (Domantas_Z), 94 (Kkgas), 97 (Elina_L), 98 (John Peacock), 100 top left (Suzyco), 100 center right (Martinturzak), 102 (Jancsikb), 104 top left (T2/Trait2Lumiere), 106 (Alan Tibbotts), 108 center right (iSampsa), 110 (Bruce Block), 112 center (Taratorki), 113 (Holgs), 114 (Jim Jurica), 116 top left (Laborer), 116 bottom right (Tella_db), 117 bottom right (Marina Dyakonova), 118 top left (Gaurti), 122 center right (Josep Pique), 124 (Bobbi Gathings), 126 top left (Alan Crawford), 128 top left (Paul Cowan), 129 (Chris Elwell), 130 bottom right (Steeve Roche), 134 top left (Howard Oates), 134 center right (Peskymonkey), 135 (Thomas Osborne), 136 (Gannet77), 138 center (John Gollop), 140 top left (Tomo Jesnicnik), 140 bottom left (Anthony Dodd), 146 (HeikeKampe), 153 bottom left (Ty Rogers), 150 (Claudia Hung), 154 (Stocksnapper), 156 top left (Samuli Siltanen), 157 bottom right (Juha Huiskonen), 158 (4kodiak); **JSMJR:** p.81; **Susannah Jayes:** p.32 bottom left; **Cha già José:** p.77 top right; **Chad K:** p.77 bottom left; **Jaan-Cornelius K:** p.12 bottom left; **Miss Karen:** p.26 top left; **John H Kim:** p.122 bottom left; **Lapplaender:** p.153 top right; **Javier Lastras:** p.18 bottom left; **Nenko Lazarov:** p.112 bottom left; **Lazlo-Photo:** p.123; **Jim Linwood:** p.67 bottom left; **Lisbon Fish and Flavours:** p.15 top right; **Lubjnx:** p.48 top left; **MC/Manuel:** p.58 top left; **Mariuszjbie:** p.88 top left; **Mattes:** p.64 top left; **Moody75:** p.1; **William Murphy:** p.55 bottom left; **Myrabella:** p.49; **Parva Farm Vineyard:** p.131 bottom right; **Gilles Paveau:** p.36 top left; **Pernak:** p.80 top left; **Rdavout:** p.30 bottom left; **RGTPR:** p.100 bottom left; **Dainee Ranaweera:** p.145; © **Copyright Kiran Ridley 2008:** pp.130 top left, 131 top left; **Shutterstock:** p.86 (Petoo); **Siesfeldt:** p.108 top left; **Peter Siroki:** p.76; **Brian Snelson:** p.9; **Jessica Spengler:** p.139; **Square Pie Ltd:** p.132 top right; **Becky Stern:** p.8; **Stockfood:** p.67 top right (Walter Pfisterer); **Stock.xchng:** back cover left (Nathalie Dulex), back cover centre (Erik Dungan), pp.14 bottom right (Paulo Simão), 18 top left (Álvaro Germán Vilel), 24 top left (Gabriel de Frietas), 34 bottom right (H Dominique Abed), 38 center (Gerd Marstedt), 42 centre right (Nathalie Dulex), 58 center (Andrea Kratzenberg), 70 center right (Stefan Otto), 82 (Luca Baroncini), 117 top right (Erik Dungan), 118 bottom left (Michel Collot), 119 (Konstantinos Dafalias), 132 center (Carl Radcliffe); **Su-Lin:** p.54; **John Sullivan:** pp.34 top left, 112 top left; **Taste of Sweden:** p.152 bottom left (Peter Backman); **Taylor's Port:** p.12 top left; **TCC:** p.144 top left; **Tourismus Salzburg GmbH:** pp.3 top center, 75 top and center right; **Titanium22:** p.42 top left; **Aurelijus Valiesa:** p.93 bottom right; **Visit OSLO:** pp.148 top left (Nancy Bundt), 149 top left (Normanns Kunstforlag/Terje Bakke Pettersen); **Paul van der Werf:** p.47; **Wieliczka Salt Mines (www.kopalnia.eu):** p.88 bottom left; **Yellow Cat:** p.18 center right; **Yisris:** p.32 top left and center right; **Robert Young:** p.10; **Manuel Zaaera:** p.20 top left; **Meg Zimbeck:** pp.46 center, 59; **Zotter:** p.74 bottom left.

CAPTIONS

Pg 1: The bustling market in Aix-en-Provence.
Pg 2 left to right: Fresh Finnish bread, famous "Salzburger Nockerl," Finnish meat.

Published in North America by Globe Pequot Press, Guilford, Connecticut

First published as *The Food Lover's Guide to Europe* in 2011 by New Holland Publishers (UK) Ltd
London • Cape Town • Sydney • Auckland

www.newhollandpublishers.com

Garfield House, 86–88 Edgware Road, London W2 2EA, United Kingdom

80 McKenzie Street, Cape Town 8001, South Africa

Unit 1, 66 Gibbes Street, Chatswood, NSW 2067, Australia

218 Lake Road, Northcote, Auckland, New Zealand

US ISBN 978-0-7627-7374-9

Publisher: Guy Hobbs
Project editor: Clare Hubbard
Editor: Richard Rosenfeld
Designer: Isobel Gillan
Picture research: Susannah Jayes
Cartography: Stephen Dew
Production: Marion Storz

Reproduction by Modern Age Repro House Ltd, Hong Kong
Printed and bound by Tien Wah Press (Pte) Ltd, Singapore

Although the publishers have made every effort to ensure that information contained in this book was researched and correct at the time of going to press, they accept no responsibility for any inaccuracies, loss, injury or inconvenience sustained by any person using this book as reference.